At ✳ Issue

Legalizing Drugs

Stuart A. Kallen, *Book Editor*

Bruce Glassman, *Vice President*
Bonnie Szumski, *Publisher*
Helen Cothran, *Managing Editor*

GREENHAVEN PRESS

An imprint of Thomson Gale, a part of The Thomson Corporation

THOMSON
✳
™
GALE

Detroit • New York • San Francisco • San Diego • New Haven, Conn.
Waterville, Maine • London • Munich

For more information, contact
Greenhaven Press
27500 Drake Rd.
Farmington Hills, MI 48331-3535
Or you can visit our Internet site at http://www.gale.com

LIBRARY OF CONGRESS CATALOGING-IN-PUBLICATION DATA

Legalizing drugs / Stuart A. Kallen, book editor.
   p. cm. — (At issue)
Includes bibliographical references and index.
   ISBN 0-7377-2408-0 (lib. : alk. paper) — ISBN 0-7377-2409-9 (pbk. : alk. paper)
    1. Drug legalization—United States. I. Kallen, Stuart A., 1955– . II. At issue (San Diego, Calif.)
HV5825.L4394 2006
363.45'0973—dc22
                                       2005046061

MAR   2007

Contents

Introduction

People have been taking drugs for most of human history. Marijuana was first cultivated over six thousand years ago. The opium poppy, the source for opiates such as morphine and heroin, was first grown by the Sumerians in present-day Iraq in 3500 B.C. The indigenous people of South America have been chewing coca leaves, the basis for cocaine, since at least 3000 B.C. Other drugs, such as LSD and MDMA, or Ecstasy, were first synthesized in the twentieth century. Throughout history such substances have been venerated as a means to spiritual enlightenment, vilified as a scourge on society, prescribed as medicines, and cursed as poisons.

Conflicting attitudes about drugs fuels controversy over drug legalization. Proponents of legalizing drugs argue that punishment for drug possession is often too severe and that government has no right to regulate personal behaviors such as drug use. Proponents and prohibitionists alike agree that drugs can cause great physical and mental damage to users. Proponents, however, believe that the number of serious abusers is relatively small (less than 3 percent in the United States) and would not skyrocket if drugs were made legal. Prohibitionists, on the other hand, fear that legalizing drugs would result in higher rates of addiction, especially among the young, causing serious harm to society.

Today, the prohibitionist viewpoint is dominant among those holding political power in the United States. It is a felony to possess, sell, or produce opiates, cocaine, Ecstasy, and many other drugs identified as "controlled substances." Depending on the amount of drugs involved, punishments range from fines and suspended sentences to life in prison with no parole.

Those who think drugs should be legalized point to incarceration rates as evidence that the war on drugs is too punitive. In 2003 state and federal police agencies in the United States arrested a record 1,678,192 U.S. citizens for drug violations. About 755,187 of those arrests, about 45 percent, were for growing, possessing, selling, or conspiring to sell marijuana. Drug legalization proponents claim that marijuana arrests alone far exceeded the

5

total number of arrests for all violent crimes combined, including murder, manslaughter, forcible rape, robbery, and aggravated assault. Of the 2 million men and women in local, state, and federal penitentiaries, about 500,000, or 25 percent were convicted on drug charges. Incarcerating drug offenders costs taxpayers $1.8 billion annually, according to most analysts.

Legalization proponents also point out that America's prison population is mostly composed of African Americans, Hispanics, and Native Americans. For example, African Americans, about 12 percent of the U.S. population, account for nearly half of the prison population, and they comprise a majority of those arrested and jailed for drug-related offenses. Such arrest rates have had a negative impact on black communities, many commentators argue. According to a 2002 Justice Policy Institute study,

> The jailing of so many young men (and increasingly women) at the primary age of family formation stunts the vitality of the black community and contributes to family dissolution, single-parent households, increased incidence of HIV/AIDS, reduced job prospects and political participation.

Concern over such unintended social costs of the drug war fuels the politically active drug legalization movement in the United States. Those who favor legalization also point out that the war on drugs seems to be having very little effect on drug use, especially in proportion to the tens of billions of dollars that have been poured into it. For example, they point out, the death toll from drugs has stayed about the same over the past thirty years.

Those who oppose drug legalization do not dispute such statistics. However, they claim that drug use would be much greater without the war on drugs. Those analysts believe that the demand for drugs, especially cocaine, has been significantly reduced by tough sentencing along with efforts to educate the public, especially the young, about the dangers of addiction. In 2002 former Drug Enforcement Administration director Asa Hutchinson told an audience in Waco, Texas:

> We've reduced casual use, chronic use, and prevented others from even starting. Overall drug use in the United States is down by half since the late 1970s. That's nine and a half million people fewer using drugs today on a regular basis than 20 years ago. . . . We've reduced cocaine use by an astound-

ing 70 percent during the last 15 years. That's over four million people fewer using cocaine on a regular basis today than 15 years ago. Those numbers represent real lives. Those are people in our families, our neighborhoods, and our communities.

To absolute prohibitionists, such reports of progress in reducing drug use show that the drug war is effective. They believe that the legalization of drugs like marijuana and cocaine would increase the incidence of drug addiction, child abuse and neglect, and workplace and traffic accidents. According to Richard M. Sloan, president of the California Narcotics Officers' Association, such results would be catastrophic for society: "There would be no greater threat to destroy our country from within than making drugs inexpensive, available and legal. [Defeat in] the war on drugs could signal the deterioration of the United States."

Prohibitionists such as Sloan continue to support the work of the Drug Enforcement Administration, which spent more than $21 billion in 2004 to stop drug production and arrest users and distributors. With so large a budgetary commitment from the federal government, it is likely that efforts to prevent Americans from acquiring and using illicit drugs will continue in the foreseeable future.

1
Federal Drug Prohibition Should Be Repealed

David Boaz and Timothy Lynch

David Boaz is the executive vice president and Timothy Lynch is the director of the Cato Institute, a libertarian think tank that opposes drug prohibition while promoting principles of limited government, individual liberty, and free markets.

Congress has no authority to prohibit individuals from smoking marijuana or using heroin, cocaine, ecstasy, or any other drug. Congress should repeal the Controlled Substances Act of 1970, which is the legal foundation of the government's war against drugs. Congress should also mandate that the Drug Enforcement Administration (DEA) respect state initiatives in California, Arizona, and elsewhere that have legalized the use of medical marijuana. Finally, Congress should stop funding the DEA, an agency that has spent hundreds of billions of taxpayer dollars on the war on drugs, only to find that levels of drug use in the United States have remained about the same for the past twenty years.

O urs is a federal republic. The federal government has only the powers granted to it in the Constitution. And the United States has a tradition of individual liberty, vigorous civil society, and limited government. Identification of a problem does not mean that the government ought to undertake to solve

David Boaz and Timothy Lynch, "Cato Handbook for Congress: Policy Recommendations for the 108th Congress," www.cato.org, January 16, 2003. Copyright © 2003 by The Cato Institute. Reproduced by permission.

it, and the fact that a problem occurs in more than one state does not mean that it is a proper subject for federal policy.

Perhaps no area more clearly demonstrates the bad consequences of not following such rules than does drug prohibition. The long federal experiment in prohibition of marijuana, cocaine, heroin, and other drugs has given us crime and corruption combined with a manifest failure to stop the use of drugs or reduce their availability to children.

In the 1920s Congress experimented with the prohibition of alcohol. On February 20, 1933, a new Congress acknowledged the failure of alcohol prohibition and sent the Twenty-First Amendment to the states. Congress recognized that Prohibition had failed to stop drinking and had increased prison populations and violent crime. By the end of 1933, national Prohibition was history, though many states continued to outlaw or severely restrict the sale of liquor.

[In 2003] Congress confronts a similarly failed prohibition policy. Futile efforts to enforce prohibition have been pursued even more vigorously in the 1980s and 1990s than they were in the 1920s. Total federal expenditures for the first 10 years of Prohibition amounted to $88 million—about $733 million in 1993 dollars. Drug enforcement costs about $19 billion a year now in federal spending alone.

Those billions have had some effect. Total drug arrests are now more than 1.5 million a year. Since 1989 more people have been incarcerated for drug offenses than for all violent crimes combined. There are now about 400,000 drug offenders in jails and prisons, and more than 60 percent of the federal prison population consists of drug offenders.

> *The long federal experiment in prohibition of marijuana, cocaine, heroin, and other drugs has given us crime and corruption combined with a manifest failure to stop the use of drugs.*

Yet, as was the case during Prohibition, all the arrests and incarcerations haven't stopped the use and abuse of drugs, or the drug trade, or the crime associated with black-market transactions. Cocaine and heroin supplies are up; the more our Customs agents interdict, the more smugglers import. And most tragic, the crime rate has soared. Despite the good news about crime in the past few years, crime rates remain at unprecedented levels.

> ❝Since 1989 more people have been incarcerated for drug offenses than for all violent crimes combined.❞

As for discouraging young people from using drugs, the massive federal effort has largely been a dud. Despite the soaring expenditures on anti-drug efforts, about half the students in the United States in 1995 tried an illegal drug before they graduated from high school. Every year from 1975 to 1995, at least 82 percent of high school seniors said they found marijuana "fairly easy" or "very easy" to obtain. During that same period, according to federal statistics of dubious reliability, teenage marijuana use fell dramatically and then rose significantly, suggesting that cultural factors have more effect than the "war on drugs."

The manifest failure of drug prohibition explains why more and more people—from Nobel laureate Milton Friedman to conservative columnist William F. Buckley Jr., former secretary of state George Shultz, Minnesota governor Jesse Ventura, and New Mexico governor Gary Johnson—have argued that drug prohibition actually causes more crime and other harms than it prevents.

Repeal the Controlled Substances Act

The United States is a federal republic, and Congress should deal with drug prohibition the way it dealt with alcohol prohibition. The Twenty-First Amendment did not actually legalize the sale of alcohol; it simply repealed the federal prohibition and returned to the several states the authority to set alcohol policy. States took the opportunity to design diverse liquor policies that were in tune with the preferences of their citizens. After 1933 three states and hundreds of counties continued to practice prohibition. Other states chose various forms of alcohol legalization.

The single most important law that Congress must repeal is

the Controlled Substances Act of 1970. That law is probably the most far-reaching federal statute in American history, since it asserts federal jurisdiction over every drug offense in the United States, no matter how small or local in scope. Once that law is removed from the statute books, Congress should move to abolish the Drug Enforcement Administration and repeal all of the other federal drug laws.

There are a number of reasons why Congress should end the federal government's war on drugs. First and foremost, the federal drug laws are constitutionally dubious. As previously noted, the federal government can exercise only the powers that have been delegated to it. The Tenth Amendment reserves all other powers to the states or to the people. However misguided the alcohol prohibitionists turned out to have been, they deserve credit for honoring our constitutional system by seeking a constitutional amendment that would explicitly authorize a national policy on the sale of alcohol. Congress never asked the American people for additional constitutional powers to declare a war on drug consumers. That usurpation of power is something that few politicians or their court intellectuals wish to discuss.

> **" The federal government spends some $19 billion to enforce the drug laws every year—all to no avail. "**

Second, drug prohibition creates high levels of crime. Addicts commit crimes to pay for a habit that would be easily affordable if it were legal. Police sources have estimated that as much as half the property crime in some major cities is committed by drug users. More dramatic, because drugs are illegal, participants in the drug trade cannot go to court to settle disputes, whether between buyer and seller or between rival sellers. When black-market contracts are breached, the result is often some form of violent sanction, which usually leads to retaliation and then open warfare in the streets.

Our capital city, Washington, D.C., has become known as the "murder capital" even though it is the most heavily policed city in the United States. Make no mistake about it, the annual carnage that accounts for America's still shockingly high murder rates has little to do with the mind-altering effects of a marijuana cigarette or a crack pipe. It is instead one of the grim and bitter consequences of an ideological crusade whose proponents will not yet admit defeat.

Third, since the [terrorist attacks] of September 11, 2001, U.S. intelligence officials have repeatedly warned us of further terrorist attacks. Given that danger, it is a gross misallocation of law enforcement resources to have federal police agents surveilling [medical] marijuana clubs in California when they could be helping to discover sleeper cells of terrorists on U.S. territory. The Drug Enforcement [Administration] has 9,000 agents, intelligence analysts, and support staff. Their skills would be much better used if those people were redeployed to full-time counterterrorism investigations.

> **// More than 70 percent of U.S. cancer specialists in one survey said they would prescribe marijuana if it were legal. //**

Fourth, drug prohibition is a classic example of throwing money at a problem. The federal government spends some $19 billion to enforce the drug laws every year—all to no avail. For years drug war bureaucrats have been tailoring their budget requests to the latest news reports. When drug use goes up, taxpayers are told the government needs more money so that it can redouble its efforts against a rising drug scourge. When drug use goes down, taxpayers are told that it would be a big mistake to curtail spending just when progress is being made. Good news or bad, spending levels must be maintained or increased.

Fifth, drug prohibition channels more than $40 billion a year into the criminal underworld occupied by an assortment of criminals, corrupt politicians, and, yes, terrorists. Alcohol prohibition drove reputable companies into other industries or out of business altogether, which paved the way for mobsters to make millions in the black market. If drugs were legal, organized crime would stand to lose billions of dollars, and drugs would be sold by legitimate businesses in an open marketplace.

Drug prohibition has created a criminal subculture in our inner cities. The immense profits to be had from a black-market business make drug dealing the most lucrative endeavor for many people, especially those who care least about getting on the wrong side of the law.

Drug dealers become the most visibly successful people in inner-city communities, the ones with money and clothes and cars. Social order is turned upside down when the most successful people in a community are criminals. The drug war makes peace and prosperity virtually impossible in inner cities.

Students of American history will someday ponder the question of how today's elected officials could readily admit to the mistaken policy of alcohol prohibition in the 1920s but recklessly pursue a policy of drug prohibition. Indeed, the only historical lesson that recent presidents and Congresses seem to have drawn from Prohibition is that government should not try to outlaw the sale of booze. One of the broader lessons that they should have learned is this: prohibition laws should be judged according to their real-world effects, not their promised benefits. If the Congress will subject the federal drug laws to that standard, it will recognize that the drug war is not the answer to problems associated with drug use.

Respect State Initiatives

The failures of drug prohibition are becoming obvious to more and more Americans. A particularly tragic consequence of the stepped-up war on drugs is the refusal to allow sick people to use marijuana as medicine. Prohibitionists insist that marijuana is not good medicine, or at least that there are legal alternatives to marijuana that are equally good. Those who believe that individuals should make their own decisions, not have their decisions made for them by Washington bureaucracies, would simply say that that's a decision for patients and their doctors to make. But in fact there is good medical evidence of the therapeutic value of marijuana—despite the difficulty of doing adequate research on an illegal drug. A National Institutes of Health panel concluded that smoking marijuana may help treat a number of conditions, including nausea and pain. It can be particularly effective in improving the appetite of AIDS and cancer patients. The drug could also assist people who fail to respond to traditional remedies.

More than 70 percent of U.S. cancer specialists in one survey said they would prescribe marijuana if it were legal; nearly half said they had urged their patients to break the law to acquire the drug. The British Medical Association reports that nearly 70 percent of its members believe marijuana should be available for therapeutic use. Even President George Bush's Office of National Drug Control Policy [ONDCP] criticized the Department of Health and Human Services for closing its special medical marijuana program. Whatever the actual value of medical marijuana, the relevant fact for federal policymakers is that in 1996 the voters of California and Arizona authorized physicians licensed in those states to recommend the use of medical marijuana to seriously ill and terminally ill patients residing in the states, without being subject to civil and criminal penalties.

> **Treat marijuana, cocaine, and heroin the way most states now treat alcohol: It should be legal for stores to sell such drugs to adults.**

It came as no surprise when the Clinton administration responded to the California and Arizona initiatives by threatening to bring federal criminal charges against any doctor who recommended medicinal marijuana or any patient who used such marijuana. After all, President Clinton and his lawyers repeatedly maintained that no subject was beyond the purview of federal officialdom.

President Bush, on the other hand, has spoken of the importance of the constitutional principle of federalism. Shortly after his inauguration, Bush said, "I'm going to make respect for federalism a priority in this administration." Unfortunately, the president's actions have not matched his words. Federal police agents and prosecutors continue to raid medical marijuana clubs in California and Arizona. And both of the president's drug policy officials, Drug Czar [ONDCP head] John Walters and DEA Chief Asa Hutchinson, have been using their offices to meddle in state and local politics. If it is inappropriate for governors and mayors to entangle themselves in foreign policy—and it is—it is also inappropriate for federal officials to entangle themselves in state and local politics. . . .

One of the benefits of a federal republic is that different policies may be tried in different states. One of the benefits of our Constitution is that it limits the power of the federal government to impose one policy on the several states.

Repeal Mandatory Minimums

The common law in England and America has always relied on judges and juries to decide cases and set punishments. Under our modern system, of course, many crimes are defined by the legislature, and appropriate penalties are defined by statute. However, mandatory minimum sentences and rigid sentencing guidelines shift too much power to legislators and regulators who are not involved in particular cases. They turn judges into clerks and prevent judges from weighing all the facts and circumstances in setting appropriate sentences. In addition, mandatory minimums for nonviolent first-time drug offenders result in sentences grotesquely disproportionate to the gravity of the offenses.

Rather than extend mandatory minimum sentences to further crimes, Congress should repeal mandatory minimums and let judges perform their traditional function of weighing the facts and setting appropriate sentences.

Restore Authority to States

Drug abuse is a problem for those involved in it and for their families and friends. But it is better dealt with as a moral and medical than as a criminal problem—"a problem for the surgeon general, not the attorney general," as former Baltimore mayor Kurt Schmoke puts it. . . .

Congress should repeal the Controlled Substances Act of 1970, shut down the Drug Enforcement Administration, and let the states set their own policies with regard to currently illegal drugs. They would do well to treat marijuana, cocaine, and heroin the way most states now treat alcohol: It should be legal for stores to sell such drugs to adults. Drug sales to children, like alcohol sales to children, should remain illegal. Driving under the influence of drugs should be illegal.

With such a policy, Congress would acknowledge that our current drug policies have failed. It would restore authority to the states, as the Founders envisioned. It would save taxpayers' money. And it would give the states the power to experiment with drug policies and perhaps devise more successful rules.

Repeal of prohibition would take the astronomical profits out of the drug business and destroy the drug kingpins who terrorize parts of our cities. It would reduce crime even more dramatically than did the repeal of alcohol prohibition. Not only would there be less crime; reform would also free federal agents to concentrate on terrorism and espionage and free local police agents to concentrate on robbery, burglary, and violent crime.

The war on drugs has lasted longer than Prohibition, longer than the Vietnam War. But there is no light at the end of this tunnel. Prohibition has failed, again, and should be repealed, again.

2

Proponents for Legalization Ignore the Harmful Effects of Drugs

James A. Inciardi

James A. Inciardi is the director of the Center for Drug and Alcohol Studies at the University of Delaware, where he is a professor in the Department of Sociology and Criminal Justice. Inciardi also is a member of the Internal Policy Committee, Executive Office of the President, Office of National Drug Control Policy.

Opponents of drug prohibition have been criticizing the war on drugs for years. Yet, while calling for drugs to be legalized and regulated like alcohol and tobacco, they have not offered concrete proposals for legalization. Many questions remain on this complex issue, such as whether or not the government should run retail stores that sell opium, crack cocaine, and LSD, or whether these dangerous substances should be sold by privately owned businesses, as alcoholic beverages are sold in liquor stores. Questions such as these have been largely unanswered by legalization proponents. And although antiprohibitionists claim widespread support, most people cannot imagine a society where dangerous and addictive drugs will be made available to anyone. Drug legalization would have a devastating effect on the social order and serious consequences for users and their families. Unless drug proponents can explain how legalization would improve society, it is necessary and proper that drugs remain illegal.

At a meeting of the U.S. Conference of Mayors in 1988, Baltimore Mayor Kurt L. Schmoke called for a national debate on U.S. drug control strategies and on potential benefits of legalizing marijuana, heroin, cocaine, crack, and other illicit substances. Schmoke's argument was that for generations the United States had been pursuing policies of prosecution and repression that resulted in little more than overcrowded courts and prisons, increased profits for drug traffickers, and higher rates of addiction.

Schmoke's comments certainly did not pass unnoticed. From a broad assortment of metaphorical garrets and cloisters and cellars and towers responses came—from a highly vocal minority of academicians and attorneys, editors and economists, and liberals and libertarians, capped by a fragmentary sampling of Marxist criminologists, blue-chip conservatives, and marijuana smokers and enthusiasts. There they were, all sharing the same podium. It was a curious mixture, like an odd and mismatched arrangement of roses, dandelions, ornamental grasses, and shaggy weeds crowded into a small rooftop flower garden. They captured the attention of the television networks, *Time* and *Newsweek*, the major dailies, House and Senate committees, the TV talk-show circuit, and even [talk show hosts Phil] Donahue and Geraldo [Rivera].

The drug legalization debate received considerable attention in 1988 and 1989, but in the years hence interest in the topic (or at least media coverage of it) has dwindled. At the same time, many former supporters of legalization moved on to embrace philosophies of decriminalization and harm reduction, approaches to the drug problem that have different meanings to different people, and terms that are often considered euphemisms for *legalization*. What do these terms mean, and are these approaches good ideas?

The Professed Benefits

Arguments posed by the supporters of drug legalization seem all too logical. First, they argue, drug laws have created evils far worse than the drugs themselves, namely, corruption, violence, street crime, and disrespect for the law. Second, legislation passed to control drugs has failed to reduce demand. Third, it is impracticable to make illegal that which a significant segment of the population in any society is committed to doing. You simply cannot arrest, prosecute, and punish such large numbers of people, particularly in a free society, a democracy. In a liberal democracy the government must not interfere with personal behavior if liberty is to be maintained. Fourth, legalizing marijuana, cocaine, crack, heroin, methamphetamine, Ecstasy, and other drugs would result in a number of positive outcomes:

1. Drug prices would fall.
2. Users could obtain their drugs at low, government-regulated prices and would no longer be forced to engage in prostitution, burglaries, robberies and muggings, and other street crimes to support their habits.
3. Levels of drug-related crime would significantly decline, resulting in less crowded courts, jails, and prisons, and freeing law enforcement personnel to focus their energies on the real criminals in society.
4. Drug production, distribution, and sale would be removed from the criminal arena; no longer would it be within the province of organized crime, and criminal syndicates such as the Colombian cartels and the Jamaican posses would be decapitalized, eliminating the violence associated with drug distribution rivalries.
5. Government corruption and intimidation by traffickers as well as drug-based foreign policies would be effectively reduced, if not eliminated entirely.
6. The often draconian measures undertaken by police to enforce the drug laws would be curtailed, thus restoring to the public many of its hard-won civil liberties.

To these contentions can be added the argument that legalization in any form or structure would have only a minimal impact on current drug-use levels. Apparently, those favoring drug legalization assume that, given the existing levels of access to most illegal drugs, current levels of use closely match demand. Thus, no additional health, safety, behavioral, and/or other problems would accompany legalization. Finally, a few proponents of legalization make one concluding point. Through government regulation of drugs, the billions of dollars spent annually on drug enforcement could be better used. Moreover, by taxing government-regulated drugs, revenues would be collected that could be used for preventing drug abuse and treating those harmed by drugs.

In the long and the short, the argument for legalization seems to boil down to the basic belief that U.S. prohibitions against marijuana, cocaine, heroin, and other drugs impose far too great a cost in terms of tax dollars, crime, and infringements on civil rights and individual liberties. Although the overall argument may be well intended and seem quite logical, it is highly questionable in its historical, sociocultural, and empirical underpinnings, and demonstrably naive in its understanding of the negative consequences of a legalized drug market.

Unresolved Issues

At the outset, it can be argued that current proposals to legalize drugs are not proposals at all. Although legalizing drugs has been debated ever since the passage of the Harrison Act [which regulated opiates and cocaine] in 1914, never has an advocate of the position structured a concrete proposal. Any attempt to legalize drugs would be extremely complex, but proponents tend to proceed from somewhat simplistic shoot-from-the-hip positions without first developing any sophisticated proposals. Even amid the clamor for legalization in the late 1980s and 1990s, specific proposals that addressed all the complex control issues could not be found. In this regard, many questions need to be addressed, including

1. Which drugs should be legalized? Marijuana? Heroin? Cocaine? If cocaine is designated for legalization, should proposals include coca products such as crack and freebase cocaine? Should the list include basuco (coca paste), that potent and highly toxic processing derivative of the coca leaf. . . . Other drugs must be considered as well. Which hallucinogenic drugs should be legalized? LSD? Peyote? Mescaline? Should Quaaludes be returned to the legal market? Should Ecstasy and the other popular club drugs be included? In short, which drugs should be legalized, according to what criteria, and who should determine the criteria?

2. Assuming that some rationally determined slate of drugs could be designated for legalization, what potency levels should be permitted? For example, 80-, 100-, and 151-proof rum; marijuana with 5, 10, and 14 percent THC content? Should legalized heroin be restricted to Burmese No. 3 grade, or should Mexican black tar and the mythical China White be added to the ledger?

3. As with alcohol, should age limits determine who can and cannot use drugs? Should those old enough to drive be permitted to buy and use drugs? Which drugs? Should sixteen-year-olds be permitted to buy pot and Quaaludes, but have to wait until age eighteen to buy cocaine and crack, and age twenty-one for heroin?

4. Should certain drugs be limited to those only who are already dependent on them? In other words, should heroin sales be restricted to heroin addicts and cocaine sales to cocaine addicts? If this approach were deemed viable, what would we say to the heroin users who want to buy cocaine? In other words, do we legalize heroin and cocaine sales but forbid speedballing [taking heroin and cocaine together]? What about drug experimenters? Should they be permitted access to the legal drug market? Assuming that these issues could be decided, in what amounts could users—regardless of their drugs of choice—purchase heroin, cocaine, marijuana, Quaaludes, and other chemical substances?

5. Where should drugs be sold? Over the counter in drug and grocery stores as is the case with many pharmaceuticals? Through mail-order houses? In special vending machines strategically located in public restrooms, hotel lobbies, and train and bus stations where cigarettes and condoms are dispensed? In tax-supported drug shacks as Representative Charles Rangel (Democrat–New York) satirically asked some years ago? Should some, or all, of the newly legalized drugs be available only on a prescription basis? If this were the case, would a visit to a physician be necessary to obtain a prescription? For how many tabs, lines, lids, bags, rocks, or whatever, should prescriptions be written? How often should these prescriptions be refillable?

> *Proponents [of drug legalization] tend to proceed from somewhat simplistic shoot-from-the-hip positions without first developing any sophisticated proposals.*

6. Where should the raw material for the drugs originate? Would cultivation be restricted to U.S. lands, or would foreign sources be permitted? Coca from Bolivia and Peru, or from all of South America and Java, as well? Marijuana from Colombia and Jamaica? Opium from Colombia, Mexico, Laos, Thailand, or from the Golden Crescent countries of Iran, Afghanistan, and Pakistan? Should trade restrictions of any type be imposed—by drug, amount, potency, purity, or by country? Should legalization policies permit the introduction of currently little-known

drugs of abuse into the United States from foreign ports. . . .

7. If drugs are to be legalized, should the drug market be a totally free one, with private industry establishing the prices as well as levels of purity and potency? What kinds of advertising should be permitted? Should advertisements for some drugs but not others be allowed? Should [celebrities who have used drugs] like Whitney Houston, Darryl Strawberry, Charlie Sheen, and Robert Downey, Jr., be permitted to endorse certain drugs or brands of drugs as part of advertising programs?

8. If drugs are to be legalized, what types of restrictions should be placed on their use? Should transportation workers, nuclear plant employees, or other categories of workers be forbidden to use them at all times, or just while they are on duty?

> *As with coffee and cigarette breaks, should users be permitted pot and coke breaks as part of their union contracts or management/labor policies?*

9. As is the case with alcohol, will certain establishments be permitted to serve drugs (and which drugs) to their customers? And similarly, as is the case with cigarettes, should there be separate drug-using and nondrug-using sections in restaurants, on planes and trains, and in the workplace? As with coffee and cigarette breaks, should users be permitted pot and coke breaks as part of their union contracts or management/labor policies?

10. For any restrictions placed on sales, potency levels, distribution, prices, quantity, and advertising in a legalized drug market, which government bureaucracy should be charged with the enforcement of the legalization statutes? The Federal Bureau of Investigation (FBI)? The Drug Enforcement Administration (DEA)? The Food and Drug Administration (FDA)? The Bureau of Alcohol, Tobacco, and Firearms (ATF)? State and local law enforcement agencies? Or should some new federal bureaucracy be created for the purpose? Going further, what kinds of penalties ought to be established for violation of the legalization restrictions?

This list is by no means exhaustive and many more questions are likely, questions both sarcastic and sardonic. But they are intended to make a point—that the whole idea of even articulating a legalization policy is very complex. Not only have proponents failed to answer the questions, but they have yet to even pose most of them. Moreover, those attempting to structure a serious proposal highlighting the beneficial expectations of a legalization policy will find little support for their arguments in either published research data or clinical experience. By contrast, numerous legitimate arguments against the legalization of drugs have considerable empirical, historical, pharmacological, and/or clinical support.

A Host of Problems

Considerable evidence suggests that the legalization of drugs would create behavioral and public health problems to a degree that would far outweigh the current consequences of the drug prohibition. There are some excellent reasons why marijuana, cocaine, crack, heroin, and other drugs are now controlled, and why they ought to remain so.

Marijuana. Considerable misinformation exists concerning marijuana. To the millions of adolescents and young adults who were introduced to the drug during the social revolution of the 1960s and early 1970s, marijuana was a harmless herb of ecstasy. As the new social drug and a natural organic product, it was deemed to be far less harmful than either alcohol or tobacco. More recent research suggests, however, that marijuana smoking is a practice that combines the hazardous features of both tobacco and alcohol with a number of pitfalls of its own. Moreover, many questions about marijuana's effect on the vital systems of the body, on the brain and mind, on immunity and resistance, and on sex and reproduction are disturbing.

One of the more serious difficulties with marijuana use relates to respiratory damage. Recent findings in this area should put to rest the rather tiresome argument by marijuana devotees that smoking just a few joints daily is less harmful than regularly smoking several times as many cigarettes. Researchers at the University of California (Los Angeles) reported in 1988 that the respiratory burden in smoke particulates and absorption of carbon monoxide from smoking just one marijuana joint is some four times greater than from smoking a single tobacco cigarette. Specifically, it was found that one toke of marijuana delivers three times more tar to the mouth and lungs than one puff of a filter-tipped cigarette; that marijuana deposits four times more tar in the throat and lungs and increases carbon monoxide levels in the blood fourfold to fivefold. Furthermore, in 1999, a National Academy of Sciences panel concluded that cellular, genetic, and human studies all suggest that marijuana smoke is an important risk factor for the development of respiratory cancer.

Marijuana apologists tend to downplay, if not totally ignore, three distinct sets of facts about its chemical structure, its persistence-of-residue effect, and its changing potency.

First, the *cannabis sativa* plant from which marijuana comes is a complex chemical factory. Marijuana contains 426 known chemicals that are transformed into 2,000 chemicals when burned during the smoking process. Seventy of these chemicals are cannabinoids, substances that are found nowhere else in nature. Because they are fat soluble, they are immediately deposited in those body tissues that have a high fat content—the brain, lungs, liver, and reproductive organs.

Second, the fact that THC (delta-9-tetrahydrocannabinol), the active ingredient and most potent psychoactive chemical in marijuana, is soluble in fat but not in water has a significant implication. The human body has a water-based waste disposal system—blood, urine, sweat, and feces. A chemical such as THC that does not dissolve in water becomes trapped, principally in the brain, lungs, liver, and reproductive organs. This is the persistence-of-residue effect. One puff of smoke from a marijuana cigarette delivers a significant amount of THC, half of which remains in the body for several weeks. As such, if a person is smoking marijuana more than once a month, the residue levels of THC are not only retained, but also building up—in the brain, lungs, liver, and reproductive organs. It is not yet clear what the long-term effects of this build-up might be.

> *Subjects used marijuana to avoid dealing with their difficulties, and the avoidance inevitably made their problems worse—on the job, at home, and in family and sexual relationships.*

Third, the potency of marijuana has risen dramatically over the years. During the 1960s the THC content of marijuana was only two-tenths of 1 percent. By the 1980s the potency of imported marijuana was up to 5 percent, representing a twenty-five-fold increase. California *sinsemilla*, on the other hand, a seedless, domestic variety of marijuana, has a THC potency of 14 percent. In fact, so potent is sinsemilla that it has become a pot of choice both inside and outside the United States. Moreover, at times sinsemilla has been traded on the streets of Bogotá, Colombia, for cocaine on an equal weight basis. Because smoked marijuana causes diminished psychomotor performance, which impairs a user's ability to operate machinery and motor vehicles, high-potency marijuana can exacerbate this effect.

> *The belief that legalizing heroin would eliminate crime, overdose, infections, and life dislocations is for the most part a mirage.*

Finally, aside from the health consequences of marijuana use, research on the behavioral aspects of the drug suggests that it severely affects the social perceptions of heavy users. Findings from the Center for Psychological Studies in New York City, for example, found that adults who smoked marijuana daily believed the drug helped them to function better—improving their self-awareness and relationships with others. In reality, however, marijuana serves as a buffer, so to speak, enabling users to tolerate problems rather than face them and make changes that might increase the quality of their social functioning and satisfaction with life. The study found that the research subjects used marijuana to avoid dealing with their difficulties, and the avoidance inevitably made their problems worse—on the job, at home, and in family and sexual relationships.

What this research documented was what clinicians had been saying for years. Personal growth evolves from learning to cope with stress, anxiety, frustration, and the many other difficulties that life presents, both small and large. Marijuana use (and the use of other drugs as well, including alcohol), particularly among adolescents and young adults, interferes with this process, and the result is a drug-induced arrested development.

Cocaine and Crack. . . . The pleasure and feelings of power that cocaine engenders make its use a rather unwise recreational pursuit. Its euphoric lift, with its feelings of pleasure, confidence, and being on top of things, that comes from but a few brief snorts is short-lived and invariably followed by a let-down. When the elation and grandiose feelings begin to wane, a corresponding deep depression is often felt that is in such marked contrast to users' previous states that they are strongly motivated to repeat the dose and restore the euphoria. This leads to chronic, compulsive use. When chronic users try to stop using cocaine, they are typically plunged into a severe depression from which only more cocaine can arouse them. Also problematic are the physiological consequences of cocaine use—convulsions, hyperstimulation, and overdose. . . .

To these can be added what is known as the cocaine psychosis. As dose and duration of cocaine use increase, the development of cocaine-related psychopathology is not uncommon. Cocaine psychosis is generally preceded by a transitional period characterized by increased suspiciousness, compulsive behavior, fault finding, and eventually paranoia. When the psychotic state is reached, individuals may experience visual and/or auditory hallucinations, with persecutory voices commonly heard. Many believe that they are being followed by police or that family, friends, and others are plotting against them. Moreover, everyday events tend to be misinterpreted in a way that support delusional beliefs. When coupled with the irritability and hyperactivity that the stimulant nature of cocaine tends to generate in almost all its users, the cocaine-induced paranoia may lead to violent behavior as a means of self-defense against imagined persecutors.

Finally, what has been said about cocaine also applies to crack . . . and perhaps more so. Crack's low price (as little as two dollars per rock in some locales) has made it an attractive drug of abuse for those with limited funds, particularly adolescents and the indigent. Its rapid absorption brings on a faster onset of dependence than is typical with cocaine, resulting in higher rates of addiction, binge use, and psychoses. The consequences include higher levels of cocaine-related violence and all the same manifestations of personal, familial, and occupational neglect that are associated with other forms of drug dependence.

Heroin. . . . The abuse liability and dependence potential of heroin is extremely high, and, historically, the drug has been associated with addiction and street crime. Although heroin overdose is not uncommon (unlike alcohol, cocaine, tobacco, and many prescription drugs), the direct physiological damage caused by heroin use tends to be minimal. For this reason the proponents of drug legalization include heroin in their arguments. By making heroin readily available to users, they argue, many problems could be sharply reduced if not totally eliminated, including the crime associated with supporting a heroin habit; the overdoses resulting from problematic levels of heroin purity and potency; the HIV and hepatitis infections brought about by the sharing of drug paraphernalia; and the personal, social, and occupational dislocations resulting from the drug-induced criminal lifestyle.

> **//** *For teenagers, drug use tended to intensify the typical adolescent problems with family and school.* **//**

The belief that legalizing heroin would eliminate crime, overdose, infections, and life dislocations is for the most part a mirage, for it is likely that the heroin-use lifestyle would change little for most users, regardless of the legal status of the drug. Ample evidence supports this argument—in biographies and autobiographies of narcotics users, in clinical assessments of heroin dependence, and in treatment literature. To this evidence can be added the many thousands of conversations conducted with heroin users over the past three decades.

The point is, heroin is a highly abusable drug. . . . Heroin becomes life consuming for those dependent on it. Because heroin is a short-acting drug, with its effects lasting at best four to six hours, it must be taken regularly and repeatedly. Because a more rapid onset occurs when taken intravenously, most heroin users inject the drug. Because heroin has depressant effects, a portion of the user's day is spent in a semistupefied state. Collectively, these effects result in a user more concerned with taking drugs than with health, family, work, or anything else.

As a final note . . . and perhaps most important, research by professors Michael D. Newcomb and Peter M. Bentler of the University of California at Los Angeles has documented the long-term behavioral effects of drug use on teenagers. Beginning in 1976 a total of 654 Los Angeles County youths were tracked for a period of eight years. Most of these youths were only occasional users of drugs and alcohol, using them moderately at social gatherings, whereas upwards of 10 percent were frequent, committed users. The impact of drugs on these frequent users was considerable. For teenagers, drug use tended to intensify the typical adolescent problems with family and school. In addition, drugs contributed to such psychological difficulties as loneliness, bizarre and disorganized thinking, and suicidal thoughts. Moreover, frequent drug users left school earlier, started jobs earlier, and formed families earlier, thus moving into adult roles with the maturity levels of adolescents. The consequences of this pattern included rapid family breakups, job instability, serious crime, and ineffective personal relationships. In short, frequent drug use prevented the acquisition of coping mechanisms that are part of maturing; it blocked teenagers' learning of interpersonal skills and general emotional development.

3

Legalizing Drugs Would Reduce Crime

Douglas N. Husak

Douglas N. Husak is professor of philosophy and law at Rutgers University and the author of Drugs and Rights *and* Philosophy of Criminal Law.

Studies have shown that illegal drug use produces three types of crime. Systemic crimes occur when drug users and dealers battle over drug sales, turf, and other aspects of illegal drug sales. Economic crimes are caused by users and addicts who steal to support their habits. Those who have psychotic, violent, or destructive episodes as a result of drug use are said to commit crimes called psychopharmacological. All three types of crimes would be reduced or eliminated if drugs were legal. Systemic crimes would be virtually eliminated if drugs were available at retail stores. Economic crimes would be unnecessary because legalization would make expensive, addictive drugs such as heroin and cocaine much more affordable. As for psychopharmacological crime, there is little proof that most drugs make people commit heinous crimes. Studies show that the majority of those who perpetrate violence under the influence of drugs are using alcohol, not illegal drugs. Contrary to the arguments of drug prohibitionists, legalizing drugs would result in less crime and would allow users to pursue their habits with much less impact on society.

Rates of violent crime in the United States are unacceptably high: Still, enormous progress has been made. The country experienced a significant reduction in crime in the 1990s. Experts disagree about why. Possible answers include overall economic prosperity, an aging population with fewer adolescents, better police work, longer sentences for violent criminals, more effective precautions by citizens and the private sector, and even the availability of safe and legal abortions (which prevented unwanted children who might have become criminals from being born). Another possible answer is the strict enforcement of laws that punish drug users. "Drug control is crime control," proclaimed Rudolph Giuliani, former mayor of New York City. . . . According to the ONDCP [Office of National Drug Control Policy] the most important objective of our drug policy—after the protection of children—is to "increase the safety of America's citizens by substantially reducing drug-related crime and violence." In this [article], I will critically respond to the rationale that crime prevention justifies our policy of punishing people who use illicit drugs for recreational purposes.

Many knowledgeable critics of this rationale would be quick to contest it on empirical grounds. Our willingness to punish illicit drug users may do little to explain the recent decline in rates of violent crime. Whether increases in the punishment of drug users coincide with decreases in violent crime depends on the year we choose as the baseline of comparison. In the 1990s, crime plummeted while punishments for drug use soared. Suppose, however, that we adopt a somewhat longer perspective, and examine these phenomena since 1980. Our prison population has tripled since 1980—much of which, . . . is due to greater punishments for drug users. Yet we now have about the same level of non-drug crime as we had then. If the punishment of drug users really were an effective means to reduce violent crime, one would expect that an increase in the former would be correlated more closely with a decrease in the latter over long periods of time.

Moreover, we should insist on getting the correct statistics before confidently proclaiming that drug use causes crime. Prohibitionists often point out that a high percentage of criminals test positive for illicit drugs. What should we conclude from this fact? The percentage of criminals who are drug users is not as meaningful as the percentage of drug users who are criminals. The latter percentage, after all, is extraordinarily low. Those who believe that drug use causes crime must struggle to explain why the vast majority of drug users never engage in criminal conduct.

Empirical misgivings aside, I am more interested in assessing whether this rationale is acceptable from the perspective of justice. In a just state, *should* we allow drug users to be punished in order to reduce violent crime? Initially, we might be tempted to answer affirmatively. In principle, crime-reduction is probably the *best* rationale for punishing illicit drug users. Everyone understands the importance of reducing violent crime. Many criminal laws that almost certainly are justified—those that punish solicitation, for example—are designed to prevent serious crime *before* it happens. Laws prohibiting drug use might be justified if they serve this same purpose. If we really succeed in preventing significant amounts of crime by punishing illicit drug users, how could any reasonable person believe that such punishments are not justified?

The Drug-Crime Connection

To evaluate this rationale, we must look more carefully at *how* and *why* the punishment of recreational drug users might be thought to reduce violent crime. In other words, we must try to understand the nature of the *drug-crime connection*. This topic is extraordinarily complex. Fortunately, social scientists have developed very powerful frameworks for understanding the link between drugs and crime. At least three types of crimes might be linked to drug use. The first types of crimes are *systemic*. Systemic crimes are those that occur because drug use is illegal and illicit drugs are bought and sold in black markets. When something goes wrong with illicit drug production or sale, buyers and sellers do not have the redress that we take for granted when a problem arises with a lawful product. If a seller cheats a buyer, or if a consumer refuses to pay a dealer, or if a user is disappointed, the complaining party can hardly go to the courthouse to file a lawsuit. Disputes of this sort must be resolved outside of normal legal channels. As a result, one would expect that illicit drug markets would be violent. Our history appears to confirm this expectation. Black markets were notoriously violent throughout the era of alcohol prohibition. Today, the black market in cocaine is comparable. The systemic crimes associated with illicit drugs include highly publicized cases of murder due to disputes involving illegal drug transactions. Sometimes, innocent children are killed in gun battles between rival drug gangs. These tragedies always give rise to calls for stricter enforcement of existing drug laws. Paradoxically, stricter enforcement can make dealing more profitable, and thereby increase the violence and incidence of the very systemic crimes it is designed to prevent.

Without question, much of the violent crime associated with illicit drugs is systemic. By most estimates, this category accounts for about 75 percent of drug-related crime. In 1988 in New York City, as many as 85 percent of crack-related crimes were caused by the market culture associated with crack sales, primarily territorial disputes between rival dealers. Decriminalization would reduce the incidence of these systemic crimes. Of course, systemic crime would be *drastically* reduced if decriminalization were extended beyond drug use to include drug production and sale. Because these systemic crimes would be decreased, even opponents of decriminalization do not always predict that it would lead to a net increase in crime. Despite his enthusiasm for prohibition, [criminal justice expert] James Q. Wilson writes: "It is not clear that enforcing the laws against drug use would reduce crime. On the contrary, crime may be caused by such enforcement." According to this school of thought, an overall increase in crime is the price we must be willing to pay for the several advantages we gain by laws that prohibit drug use.

> *Those who believe that drug use causes crime must struggle to explain why the vast majority of drug users never engage in criminal conduct.*

In my judgment, Wilson is half right and half wrong. He is probably correct to think that more crime, rather than less, is caused by our prohibition of drug use. He is incorrect, however, to conclude that the advantage that such laws allegedly produce—a significant decrease in the incidence of drug use—outweighs the disadvantage he cites. I believe that the enormous amount of systemic crime caused by prohibition is too high a price to pay for any of the speculative goods that might result from punishing drug users. Unfortunately, I cannot prove that I am correct about how these advantages and disadvantages should be balanced. . . . But I would bet that the innocent victims of systemic crimes would tend to agree with my assessment that the drawbacks outweigh the benefits. The mother of a teenage drug user killed in a confrontation with police would be stunned to learn that serious academics concede that decriminalization would have saved the life of her child, but oppose it nonetheless.

Before leaving the topic, I must point out that the phenomenon of systemic crime associated with the illicit drug trade is much more complex than appearances might suggest. First, not all black markets are especially violent. Many black markets exist in America other than illicit drug markets—such as those involving gambling. These other black markets are not notorious for their high rates of violence. Second, even black markets in drugs are not particularly violent in other countries. In Australia, for example, significantly less systemic violence is associated with drug transactions—even though rates of drug use are roughly comparable to those in the United States. Finally, much of the violence in America's illicit drug trade appears to be attributable to predispositions toward violent lifestyles that predate involvement with drugs. In other words, drug markets may not cause violence as much as attract people who were already prepared to be violent. Therefore, not all of the violence associated with the drug trade should be attributed to the fact that drug transactions are illegal. Factors peculiar to contemporary America explain this violence. When an innocent child is killed in a drive-by shooting between rival dealers, we are quick to blame the drugs, but reluctant to mention other factors—most notably, guns. These violent acts might just as well be attributed to America's "gun culture" as to our "drug culture."

Whatever the deep explanation of the systemic violence associated with illicit drugs in the United States, we must recognize that decriminalization would reduce this category of crime. This recognition puts us in a better position to decide whether selective prohibition can be justified as a means to prevent crime. The disputed and crucial issue is not simply whether drug use causes crime, but whether drug use causes criminal conduct that would persist even if drug use itself were not prohibited. When we try to assess the merits of decriminalization by analyzing the drug-crime connection, we should remember that most criminal behavior associated with drugs is not caused by drugs *per se*, but rather by the fact that drug use is illegal.

Economic Crime

This crucial point must be kept in mind as we turn our attention to the second type of crime associated with illicit drugs: *economic* crime. Drug use causes economic crime for a simple reason. Partly because of addiction, illicit drug users tend to want drugs very badly, and are willing to go to extraordinary lengths to obtain them. Many illicit drugs are expensive. This combination of strong demand and high price leads users to commit economic crimes to get the money to buy drugs. Some estimates of the number of property offenses committed by drug users are astronomical. A few experts once conjectured that virtually *all* of the economic crime in New York City was committed by heroin addicts who needed to finance their habits. Other experts replied that these estimates were wild exaggerations. Who is correct? One way to estimate the extent of economic crime committed by addicts who need money to finance their habits is to survey prison inmates convicted of economic crimes. Only about 25 percent of adult inmates who use illicit drugs and commit economic crimes cite their drug use as a primary motivation for becoming involved in criminal activity. Many such persons began committing economic crimes prior to using drugs. . . .

> *Paradoxically, stricter enforcement can make dealing more profitable, and thereby increase the violence and incidence of the very . . . crimes it is designed to prevent.*

Whatever the true extent of economic crime associated with illicit drugs, we must struggle to determine whether such crime is caused by drugs, or is caused by drug prohibitions. If less economic crime would occur under decriminalization than prohibition, the goal of reducing economic crime could hardly be the rationale for punishing drug users. Unfortunately, this question is not easy to answer. Again, the main difficulty is our lack of certainty about how illicit drugs would be bought and sold if drug users were no longer punished. Under most models of decriminalized markets, illicit drugs would be far less expensive. Some academics have estimated that heroin could be lawfully bought and sold at about 2 percent of its current, black-market price. If this estimate were roughly accurate, one would anticipate that decriminalizing the sale of heroin (and other illicit drugs) would cause a drastic reduction in economic crime. This prediction is based partly on an examination of the extent of economic crime associated with licit drugs. Alcoholics and tobacco addicts rarely steal to purchase their drugs, but not because their addictions are less powerful—but because they can afford to buy what users of illicit drugs cannot.

On the other hand, . . . drugs in decriminalized markets may *not* be significantly less expensive. The price of these drugs would depend on unknown variables like the rate of taxation. In addition, if decriminalized drugs really were less expensive, greater numbers of people might be inclined to use them. Greater numbers of users might translate into a higher population of addicts, who in turn might cause greater amounts of economic crime—even though drugs were cheaper. No one should be very confident about how the incidence of economic crime would be affected by the decriminalization of drug use. Despite this uncertainty, one point is clear. The incidence of economic crime associated with illicit drugs is not simply attributable to illicit drugs *per se*, but to complex features of drug markets—most notably, to the high price of drugs. High prices are due more to the fact that drug sales are illegal than to the cost of producing illicit drugs. If our objective is the reduction of economic crime, we are better off controlling markets and fixing the price of illicit drugs at the point at which the incidence of economic crime is minimized. There is no reason to believe that this optimal point corresponds to the cost of drugs in the black markets of today. We should be very reluctant to believe that punishing drug users is an effective way to reduce economic crime.

Drugs and Violent Behavior

The third type of crime in the drug-crime connection is *psychopharmacological*. This category of crime results from the effects of drugs themselves, rather than from the fact that their use and sale is prohibited. The use of drugs may cause violent, criminal acts in somewhat different ways. Drugs may release inhibitions that can generally be restrained. Drugs may impair judgment and perception, leading users to act in ways they would otherwise avoid. According to [former head of the Office of National Drug Control] William Bennett, "the fact is that under the influence of drugs, normal people do not act normally, and abnormal people behave in chilling and horrible ways." This account of the connection between drug use and crime is reminiscent of the story of Dr Jekyll and Mr Hyde. Dr Jekyll consumed a potion that transformed him into the homicidal Mr Hyde. The psychopharmacological effects of this potion caused an otherwise law-abiding physician to become a violent monster. Of course, this story is purely fictitious. If any existing drug resembled the potion in this story, we would have excellent reasons to criminalize its use.

Fortunately, no existing drug resembles this fictional potion. Scholars are far more ambivalent than Bennett about this explanation of the drug-crime connection. Of course, we can always fall back on anecdotes. But research provides no evidence that people under the influence of marijuana or heroin are more likely to become aggressive and violent. These drugs tend to have the opposite effect; their psychopharmacological properties cause users to become passive. Studies indicate that users of marijuana are substantially under-represented among violent criminals when researchers are careful to control for other variables such as age. The situation with cocaine is a bit less clear. Cocaine users themselves, however, report that the drug almost never leads them to commit violent acts they would not have performed otherwise. Ironically, alcohol is the drug most likely to lead to psychopharmacological crime. If we accept this rationale for punishing drug users—and prohibit drugs that cause people to become violent and aggressive—we would begin by punishing drinkers. More generally, if we propose to ban those drugs that are implicated in criminal behavior, no drug would be a better candidate for criminalization than alcohol. In 1998, the National Center on Addiction and Substance Abuse (NCASA) reported that 21 percent of persons in state jails or prisons for violent crime were under the influence of alcohol and no other drug at the time they committed their crime. Only 3 percent were under the influence of cocaine or crack alone, and 1 percent were under the influence of heroin alone. . . .

Of course, the criminal law is and ought to be in the business of protecting citizens from the risk of harm. This is why we criminalize drunk driving, for example. Obviously, only a small percentage of drunk drivers actually cause a crash. Still, drunk driving is properly criminalized because it increases the risk of a crash. Isn't the rationale for drug prohibitions comparable? . . .

I conclude that no account of the drug-crime connection provides an acceptable justification for criminalization. Because of systemic and economic crime, drug prohibition may actually cause more crime than it prevents. And even if the statistical overlap between drug use and violent criminality indicates that we could prevent some of the latter by punishing all of the former, justice would not allow us to do so.

4

Legalizing Drugs Would Not Reduce Crime

Joe Dombroski

Joe Dombroski of Richmond, Virginia, is an enforcement su-pervisor for the U.S. Drug Enforcement Administration.

Illegal drugs generate crime in many sectors of society. Users steal and rob to obtain money for drugs while dealers shoot each other in battles over territory. Drug proponents say legalization would reduce such crime by taking the profit motive out of drug sales, but this is not true. If the government were to produce drugs such as heroin, cocaine, and marijuana, the manufacturing costs would keep prices high. Addicts would still be forced to steal to support their habits and buy from street dealers, who could sell drugs more cheaply. The only way to reduce crime is through tough law enforcement.

The myth of the drug legalization argument is that government distribution/regulation of drugs would remove the profit, and therefore the incentive, for illicit drug-dealing and drug-related crime.

But the reality of drug legalization can be witnessed by any American tourist on the streets of a working-class neighborhood in southern Amsterdam. In that typical Netherlands neighborhood, residents weave on and off crowded sidewalks, trying to avoid making eye contact with dealers who openly push heroin, marijuana, and crack.

In news reports and interviews, hard-working area residents blame the legalization of drugs for bringing more drug dealers,

Joe Dombroski, "Tough Enforcement Succeeds: Record Shows That Drug Legalization Is No Solution," *Richmond Times-Dispatch*, March 16, 2003. Copyright © 2003 by Richmond Newspapers, Inc. Reproduced by permission.

more petty criminals, and more drug use to their neighborhood.

Twenty-five years ago police departments in the United States regarded drug use as a victimless crime affecting only the user. Vice enforcement treated drug crimes in the same manner as prostitution and gambling. Today law-enforcement officials understand that drug use and drug distribution are crimes with an untold number of victims. Society, as well as the drug user, suffers both physically and economically. The U.S. system of uniform crime reporting reveals that between 75 percent and 80 percent of all crime is drug-related or has a drug nexus.

Drug-Related Crimes

Legalization and government distribution/regulation do not stop the profits for illegal drug dealers. If we examine the basic economics of drug trafficking, we can understand what the people of Amsterdam are living with.

In a typical drug-producing country a kilogram (1,000 grams) of heroin sells for about $1,000. That same kilogram is then sold to wholesale dealers in the United States for between $85,000 and $100,000. In Richmond [Virginia] a street dose (1/8 gram or an "egg") of heroin sells for $25. Thus a street dealer in Richmond can make $200,000 per kilogram. Once the dealer pays his cost of $85,000 to $100,000, he will realize a profit of 100 percent or more per kilogram.

> *Law-enforcement officials understand that drug use and drug distribution are crimes with an untold number of victims.*

The government of a country with legalized drugs has to sell heroin for no less than $20 per street dose, to cover the pharmaceutical manufacturer's production costs. The government has to deliver a consistently safe strength per dose, and therefore it cannot purchase drugs as an illegal drug trafficker can. Meanwhile, the drug dealer who purchases his drugs from illicit sources that operate with no quality controls or safety standards can cut his price to $15 per street dose, underselling the government and realizing a smaller profit. He still makes money and the addicts purchase cheaper, and, in many instances, more potent heroin from the street dealers.

The attitude implicit in a culture of drug use and acceptance in the Netherlands has played an important role in its becoming the world's top supplier of Ecstasy. Legalization has produced a drug-addicted population that has crippled the economy. In the summer of 2002, the legislature of the Netherlands reversed two decades of legalized drugs by passing laws to recriminalize drug distribution and use in order to protect its citizenry.

Current Approaches Work

The current approach in our country of tough drug laws, coupled with effective education programs and compassionate treatment, is producing success. It is a myth that there has been no progress in our anti-drug efforts. Overall drug use in the U.S. has dropped by more than one-third since the late 1970s. That means 9.5 million fewer people are using illegal drugs. During the past 15 years cocaine use has plummeted by an astounding 70 percent.

There is still more to do. Drugs remain readily available, and a recent household survey on drug abuse revealed that an increasing number of American children are experimenting with designer drugs such as Ecstasy. As long as we have despair, poverty, frustration, and teenage rebellion, we're going to have problems with drugs. We must remember that our methods are achieving success. Less than 5 percent of the population—or 16 million people—regularly uses illegal drugs.

Emerging drug threats such as Ecstasy and methamphetamine will require even more resolve and innovation. We need a renewed dedication by all Americans to help our children stay away from the misery and addiction of drugs.

> *The current approach in our country of tough drug laws, coupled with effective education programs and compassionate treatment, is producing success.*

Innovative approaches to address the problem include drug courts, community coalitions such as the Richmond Drug Free Alliance, more investment in education, more effective treatment, drug-testing in the workplace, and drug counselors in schools. These ideas work. What doesn't work is legalization.

Alaska Tried Legalization

It's a well-kept secret that legalization has been tried before in this country. In 1975, Alaska's Supreme Court held that under its state constitution an adult could possess marijuana for personal consumption in the home. However, in a 1988 study, the University of Alaska found that the state's teens used marijuana at more than twice the national average for their age group. In 1990, Alaska's residents, fed up with the dangerous experiment of legalization, voted to recriminalize possession of marijuana.

Legalization was not the answer for the Netherlands or for Alaska—nor is it for the rest of America. Legalizing drugs is simply surrendering. It's giving upon the hope that future generations will be drug-free and abandoning those people in the grip of addiction. Isn't every life worth fighting for?

5

The War on Drugs Is Destroying Lives

Jack Cole

Jack Cole, a retired New Jersey state police lieutenant, had extensive experience in undercover narcotics work. He is co-founder of Law Enforcement Against Prohibition (LEAP), an organization of police, judges, and district attorneys who oppose the war on drugs and who lobby for drug legalization.

The war on drugs has been waged in the United States since Congress passed the Controlled Substances Act in 1970. In the following three and a half decades, hundreds of billions of taxpayer dollars have been spent while millions of otherwise law-abiding people have had their lives ruined after being arrested on drug charges. All the while, the percentage of Americans using illegal drugs has barely changed. Some who have worked as narcotics agents, judges, and district attorneys are aware that it is not drugs causing societal problems, but the war on drugs itself. Few people on the frontlines of the drug war believe drugs are a smart lifestyle choice. However, those who have seen the corruption of public officials, the profits generated by terrorists, and the human suffering caused by the drug war believe that the only solution is the legalization and regulation of all drugs.

Editor's note: The following viewpoint has been excerpted from a transcript of a radio interview with Jack Cole. The interview was conducted by Hamish McKenzie on Radio One in Dunedin, New Zealand, on April 26, 2004.

Jack Cole, "The War on the War on Drugs," www.leap.cc, April 26, 2004. Copyright © 2004 by Law Enforcement Against Prohibition. Reproduced by permission.

Hamish McKenzie: Now, 12 years as an undercover narcotics dealer, you must have seen some interesting things:

Jack Cole: "A few. Yes. I saw a lot of horrible things, and most of the horrible things were the things we were doing to young people by destroying their lives in this War on Drugs."

What sort of things did you see that you thought the police, or the War on Drugs, were responsible for?

"Well, the war on drugs was really responsible for about 99% of all the things that we attribute to the, quote, 'drug problem.' Which truly should be attributed to drug prohibition because it is prohibition that causes the sale of drugs to become an underground market and the fact that it's illegal artificially inflates the values of these products virtually by up to 17,000 percent increase between where they're grown, mainly, in third world countries, like, as you know, Afghanistan, Colombia, and where they're sold in Los Angeles, or New York City. . . . 17,000 percent increase—that creates an obscene profit motive, making many people willing to kill each other in the streets in order to control their little end of the market."

> **" I came to understand that this is not a war on drugs—it's a war on people. "**

So I guess you'd be of the opinion that the problems caused by the government's stance on drugs far outweigh the problems caused by drugs on the individuals themselves?

"Absolutely. Beyond any doubt. And we don't suggest that drugs are a great thing. At LEAP [Law Enforcement Against Prohibition] we think drugs are a poor choice—we just don't think people should be arrested for making that choice. You're not arrested for making a choice of drinking alcohol, or smoking tobacco, and those are the two worst drugs known to human beings. In . . . the United States, tobacco kills 430,000 people every year. Alcohol kills another 110,000—I'm not talking about people who get drunk and run off the road and kill themselves; I'm talking about just ingesting that, because it is a poison and it will get you. All the illegal drugs combined in the United States kill less than 12,000 people. So 12,000 is a lot of people, but I would suggest that any drug warrior who says that we have to continue spending 69 billion dollars—which is what we spend every year to fight the war on drugs in the United States—69 billion dollars in order to destroy the lives of the 1.6 million people we arrest for non-violent drug violations every year, in order to somehow save 12,000 lives, when we're killing 540,000 with these other two legal drugs, they're being just slightly disingenuous."

That's true. While you were in the New Jersey police force, were you committed to the cause? Did you completely believe in what you were doing?

"Well not for the whole time, but I certainly did when I joined the narcotics unit. I spent 14, almost 14 years actually, in narcotics and 12 of it actually working narcotics—the last two, . . . I was working [against] terrorists—but when I started I was absolutely convinced that drugs were the scourge of the earth. I mean, I grew up looking at things like the old [anti-drug] movie that everybody laughs at today, thank goodness, *Reefer Madness*, and *Man with the Golden Arm* [in which Frank Sinatra played a heroin addict], and all these things, and I actually believed that these were terrible drugs. I thought I didn't have drug problems, I grew up in Kansas in the middle of America, and I thought we don't have any drug problems out there. The people with drug problems are the people who might smoke a joint on a Friday night. But looking back, I had major drug problems: I used to get falling down drunk on alcohol about once a week when I was 14 with all my mates out there. And I smoked two packs of cigarettes every day for 15 years—so I had major drug problems. I just didn't realise that these things were drugs, you know."

> *[Terrorist] Osama bin Laden made almost every penny that he ever got from selling heroin out of Afghanistan mostly in the United States.*

True. So what did [you] see during that working as a narcotics officer, or what was it that changed your mind? What was it that changed your mind, changed your attitudes toward drugs, or at least the drug laws, the way they're enforced?

"You mean, was there an epiphany?"

Yeah, was there an epiphany, were there any specific incidents?

"Well, there really was an epiphany. There were several things:

The first thing that really threw me was about three years into working undercover, working with these folks, it suddenly occurred to me that I liked a lot of the people I was working on, better than the people I was working for. They seemed to be a kinder, gentler group of folks that weren't nearly as likely to stab me in the back. And I came to understand that this is not a war on drugs—it's a war on people. In the United States over 87 million people above the age of 12 have used an illegal drug—that means that this is literally a war on people. It's a war on our children, a war on our parents, a war on ourselves.". . .

Gangsters, Murderers, and Terrorists

That's some very interesting points you make there. You can't be very popular with the Bush administration.

"Ha ha, that's true."

Do you face any pressures from those quarters?

"Not so far, because I don't think we're enough of a thorn in their side yet, but certainly as we grow we will. There's no doubt we will."

Do you think that's a strong current to swim against—the [anti-drug] propaganda that the Bush administration is putting out there?

"Well sure, and they have some rather strong allies: all the drug lords also feel that these laws should exist, because if we legalise drugs today, tomorrow the drug lords and the terrorists in this world would be out of business—they wouldn't make another penny on drugs. And when I say terrorists, I really mean terrorists. You know, [terrorist] Osama bin Laden made almost every penny that he ever got from selling heroin out of Afghanistan mostly in the United States, a lot in Europe, and now coming down [to Australia and New Zealand]. It's true he was given 300 million dollars by daddy as an inheritance, which sounds like a lot to you. But think about someone fomenting wars in countries: 300 million dollars as you know won't even last a day. But if [he] took that 300 million dollars 25 years ago, as he did, and invested it solely in heroin, you'd be worth hundreds of billions of dollars today, and very well capable of fomenting wars around the world."

So you're definitely pushing regulation rather than prohibition, and when do you want to see this happen?

"Yes, and we're not just talking regulation: we like to say legalisation. And of course when the drug warriors talk about it, they say, 'Oh yeah, they want to legalise drugs so we can all go out and party. That's not the definition. The definition of legal-isation is a process whereby you can control and regulate some-thing. Right now we leave the regulation and control of drugs in the hands of all the gangsters and murderers and terrorists out there. And that's the wrong people to control drugs. And you were asking about when? Well, I would say sooner rather than later. But if we legalise drugs tomorrow, it would be too late as far as I'm concerned, because today we're going to de-stroy a lot more young lives by arresting people.". . .

A War on Constitutional Rights

What are some of the uglier things you've seen during your time as an undercover agent?

"Well I think the really ugly things that bear on my mind are the things that the police did. Because we were trained to fight a war on drugs—because of that metaphor—we felt like we had to have an enemy, and the enemy when you're trying to fight a war becomes the citizens of your country. And when you're fighting a war that's a very, very terrible metaphor for policing in a democratic society, because when you're fighting a war it's no holds barred. And the holds that we didn't have to bar anymore were the holds on our constitutional rights, which we would just stomp on. Our fourth amendment right in the United States against illegal search and seizure. We would illegally search people all the time, because we felt like 'we're fighting a war, we're the good guys, and no matter how we get these guys, it's worthwhile because we're taking them off the streets and that's our job.' So that's why so many get in-volved in not telling the truth on the stand when they're testi-fying about drug cases. And you almost never find that in other cases. All these violations come from drug cases.

For instance, you can read a whole lot of newspapers, see a whole lot of newscasts and never hear anything about anybody violating someone's rights in, say, a murder investigation, or, say, a rape investigation, but when it's drugs it's different, be-cause we're fighting a war on drugs. Because we were fighting a war the police officers thought that the courts weren't doing their jobs correctly—they used to talk about revolving door jus-tice—you know, in and out so quick—and they'd complain . . . that the criminals that they'd just arrested for a drug violation were back on the street before they could finish typing up the report—which was probably true, in many cases. But in the

United States we have the right to bail: If you make bail, you get out. So what's the matter with that? It doesn't mean you're released; it just means you're out until your court case comes up. But the police couldn't see it that way; they said they were getting out on the streets and right back to dealing. So they started applying what they called 'street justice'. And street justice meant doing any despicable thing you could to these people. The worse the better, because it was just one more reason that they wouldn't in the future dare to try using drugs again. So when we'd go in, for instance, to search a house, early on, when we started this war on drugs, we'd go in to execute a search warrant. We'd go in the house, we'd kick down all the doors, always. Whether they needed [to] be or not, you know, you just kick them in, it's just part of the street justice—they had to repair their doors. Go inside to search the house, arrest everybody in the house, turn over drawers and the beds and just break things, just as part of the search, just automatically. And its always thought of as street justice. And then if you arrested everyone in the house because you found some drugs there, when we brought them out in chains and put them in the police cars and drove off, we just left that shattered door wide open, so anybody could go and steal anything they wanted. We didn't care: that's all the more reason that they'll never do this again."

> **Street justice meant doing any despicable thing you could to these people. The worse the better.**

Did that happen? Did people go into those places?

"Oh, absolutely it happened. Certainly. And who could they go to to complain? The police? Hardly. So those were some things I felt were horrible. Horrible. We'd hit houses— and of course, mainly you're hitting the house at 5 o'clock in the morning so you're guaranteed that the people are there asleep. You go in to get some guy that's sold some drugs to someone, and the police would hit the house, kick down the door, go in, and maybe the guy that sold it is the son of the parents who live in the house. But when we went in the house, you know, we'd grab him, we'd grab everyone; everyone's down on the floor and they're handcuffed at first, until you get a chance to search the house, and secure it so nobody can get to guns and everything. Sometimes these people's mother would be naked in there. It didn't matter. Down on the floor and handcuffed. Didn't give them a chance to dress, or do anything. Just because with this kind of embarrassment, maybe they'd really keep their son from using these drugs again. So it was all these terrible things."

> **❝ There was always physical abuse. Tremendous physical abuse. ❞**

Was there ever any physical abuse?

"Oh, sure. There was always physical abuse. Tremendous physical abuse. People get slapped around all the time. And worse. About any degrading thing you can think of I saw occur out there. And it was terrible. Terrible, terrible. So that is what comes first in my mind when I think of bad things I saw out there. I saw other things out there that some of the cops said, 'Oh, this is the worse thing ever!' And this went toward fighting the war on drugs.". . .

What's going to have to happen for this war on drugs to end? Would a change in the administration help things?

"Not much, no. It's not just the Bush administration. The Clinton administration made more stringent laws. Both sides, no matter who we put in there, just buys into the War on Drugs. No, what will make the change is an organisation like LEAP. We founded our organisation and modelled it on Vietnam Veterans Against the War. This was before your time, but we believed that those people [the combat veterans] had such unassailable credibility when it came to speaking out against that horrible war, because they've been there done that: 'It's wrong and we've got to get out.' And how do you argue with someone that's been there and done that? And we feel we have exactly the same credibility when we speak out against the War on Drugs. And that's why all the speakers in LEAP, and board members, have to be current or former drug warriors, either police, judges, prosecutors—we even have former DEA [Drug Enforcement Administration] agents who are speakers for us. So there's a lot of folks out there that understand this, and it's growing every day. And this is what will make the change because as we speak to people, publicly, there's so many people out there that are on our side: They don't even know that they're on our side, until they hear what is actually happening with the War on Drugs. They hear what kind of horrors we've really created, and they say, 'This is so logical, this is so compelling an argument, naturally we have to end the drug prohibition, we have to legalise drugs.' And when we say 'legalise drugs' we don't mean party, which is what the drug warriors would have you believe: we mean legalise it so that you can control it and regulate it and keep it out of the hands of our children."

6

Arguments Against the War on Drugs Are Based on Dangerous Myths

Dan P. Alsobrooks

Dan P. Alsobrooks is a district attorney general for the Twenty-third Judicial District in Tennessee, and president of the National District Attorneys Association in Virginia.

Drug proponents are putting forth a growing number of proposals and referendums to legalize or decriminalize drugs. To support their cause, the antiprohibitionists claim that marijuana can alleviate suffering in medical patients, that nonviolent drug users are overfilling prisons, and that drugs are really not harmful to society. These are inaccurate and dangerous myths that authorities need to counter by clearly showing that the war on drugs has been having impressive positive effects. Society's acceptance of drug use has fallen along with the numbers of drug users. Despite its achievements in the drug war, law enforcement has failed to convince a large percentage of Americans to support its efforts.

Prosecutors know through experience that the majority of crimes in communities are drug-related. This is an indisputable fact, backed by incontrovertible evidence, including prosecutors' bulging caseloads. Those who seek to decriminalize drug use ignore the facts and the evidence, relying on myths to mislead the public and advance their cause.

The crimes related to substance abuse range far beyond drug

Dan P. Alsobrooks, "Waging a Battle Against Myths," *Corrections Today*, vol. 64, December 2002. Copyright © 2002 by the American Correctional Association, Inc., Lanham, MD. Reproduced by permission.

possession. They run the gamut from environmental pollution to murder. Crimes include gang wars to control drug markets; methamphetamine manufacturing sites that are a biohazard; and deaths caused by drug-impaired drivers. The list goes on.

Propositions, proposals and legislation to legalize or decriminalize controlled substances are springing up around the country. The drug legalization movement is well-funded and highly adept at manipulating the media. Unless law enforcement speaks out more forcefully, our communities will find themselves facing an onslaught of violence and death directly attributable to the use of dangerous and poisonous drugs that have previously been controlled. We face a well-financed opposition with a well-organized political machine that can outspend us state by state and referendum by referendum. Operating under umbrella groups, the opposition uses a legislative strategy akin to the death of a thousand cuts. Those who want to legalize drugs advance their position, issue by issue, winning by incremental victories, while law enforcement officials often regard such victories as isolated losses.

> *The drug legalization movement is well-funded and highly adept at manipulating the media.*

For example, in one state, a legalization referendum misleads voters to believe that the issue is alleviating suffering for cancer patients. In another state, the issue is disguised as a legislative mandate to decriminalize certain types of drug use and provide treatment programs. And in a third state, legalization efforts are an attempt to limit asset forfeiture. Each such manipulation chips away at the foundation of law enforcement's efforts to fight substance abuse throughout the nation. With each such victory, those who would undermine law enforcement grow stronger and our communities become less safe.

Waging a Battle Against Myths

More than 100 of these so-called and cleverly disguised drug policy "reforms" have been enacted in 40 states since 1996 and 41 were enacted in 2001 alone. There have been some successful efforts to reject some so-called reforms, most notably in Massachusetts and Oregon, but they remain in the minority. Those who would legalize drugs boast of their success in Nevada, where [in 2001], marijuana was decriminalized and where . . . , [in 2002] the issue on the ballot was actual legalization. . . .

> ❝ Unless law enforcement officials counter such myths and convince America that these substances are not harmless . . . they will continue to lose the fight and the legalization lobby's prophecies will come true. ❞

More ominously, those who support the drug legalization effort brag that the American people are significantly changing their opinions on drug abuse and the criminal justice system and that this "shift in public opinion" will lead to a groundswell of support for their cause. On one of the proponents' Web sites, they boldly claim, "States are reigning in the excesses of the war on drugs regardless of what the federal government is doing. Since most drug arrests occur at the state level, state reforms are having a huge impact on the lives of millions of Americans. At the rate states are reforming their drug laws, the federal government may very soon find itself alone in supporting punitive and antiquated drug policies."

Battling the Myths

A major aspect of the public relations effort to bring about the state-by-state change rests on the continual repetition of myths. This, plus the American public's lack of understanding of the real dangers of substance abuse, provides those who support legalization with a sometimes-winning media campaign. Americans appear to be in serious denial about the problems associated with drugs: It is "someone else's child"; "something that will never hurt me"; or "someone else's life that will be jeopardized, not mine." Unless law enforcement officials counter such myths and convince America that these substances are not harmless, that the criminal justice system does not ruin people's lives, but rather, dangerous and addictive drugs do, they will continue to lose the fight and the legalization lobby's prophecies will come true.

One of the most popular myths regarding drugs is that jails are filled with people who are guilty only of possession for personal use. Law enforcement officials know that this is not true. The fact is that most individuals who are found in simple possession of drugs are placed in diversion and treatment programs and that this is not a new trend. Prosecutors and the courts have long recognized that prison cells should be reserved for the worst offenders and for those who refuse to rehabilitate and reform their dangerous conduct. Unfortunately, part of the basis for this myth is a practice of some prosecutors that should be explained or changed. Too often, offenders are sent to prison as the result of a plea agreement under which a charge of selling drugs is reduced to simple possession. Additionally, offenders may be incarcerated for possession with intent to distribute a controlled substance—a very different offense than possession for personal use. Further, many offenders who have been provided with rehabilitation opportunities and probation violate the conditions of their release and leave the courts no option but to incarcerate them.

According to a study published by the New York State Department of Corrections, of the 22,000 people in jail in New York for drug crimes, 87 percent were incarcerated for selling drugs or intent to sell drugs. Of the 12 percent incarcerated for possession, 76 percent were arrested for selling drugs and pleaded down their charges to possession. Additionally, the study found that most convicted first-time drug offenders end up on probation or in drug treatment rather than in jail. Statistics from Florida are similar. According to the Florida Department of Law Enforcement, of the 1,555 inmates in prison for drug possession on July 31, 2001, none were first-time offenders.

> *Drugs are illegal because they are harmful, both to immediate users and to others who become victimized by the effects of drugs on users.*

Each state has a similar story to tell and research must be conducted and data obtained that reflect the actual basis for incarceration. Likewise, prosecutors must understand that by pleading down cases, they are, in some instances, providing ammunition to their opponents. They need to tell their many success stories—of their drug courts, their diversion and treatment programs, and their efforts at all stages in the criminal justice system to provide substance abuse treatment. Prosecutors also must inform the public that without the threat of incarceration, habitual and addicted drug offenders will not enter or complete rehabilitation programs. This is very much in accord with former President Teddy Roosevelt's axiom of speaking softly but carrying a big stick—here, prosecutors' "stick" to ensure diversion program participation is the fear of going to jail.

Harmful to Users and Victims

Another myth, popular with a culture that has advertising campaigns flouting the need to follow societal rules, is that drug abuse is a victimless crime. The use of illegal drugs is not victimless. Regretfully, nearly every family has been hurt by addiction. It has consequences that touch the lives of children and adults nationwide. The victims of drug abuse range from those physically harmed by drug-induced crimes to taxpayers footing the bill for drug treatment. In other words, every citizen is a victim, either directly or indirectly.

> *Murders related to narcotics rank as the fourth most documented murder circumstance of 24 possible categories.*

Drugs are illegal because they are harmful, both to immediate users and to others who become victimized by the effects of drugs on users. In 1999, there were 19,102 deaths from drug-induced causes (legal and illegal drugs). During that year, there were 168,763 cocaine-related emergency room episodes alone. The following year, the Substance Abuse and Mental Health Administration's Drug Abuse Warning Network reported that there were 601,563 drug-related episodes in hospital emergency rooms nationwide. Who is paying the bills for these cases? The numbers speak for themselves. Between 1992 and 1998, the overall cost of drug abuse to society increased at a rate of 5.9 percent annually. By 1998, victimless crime was costing society $143.4 billion each year for health-related expenses alone. This, however, does not include the emotional costs to those actually victimized by substance abuse: the battered spouses, victims of impaired drivers and victims of assault and rape. These costs are beyond calculation.

A third myth used to support legalization is that drug use does not impact crime rates. One must wonder whether the people who say this have ever spoken to the victim of an assailant high on drugs; to the parents of a child killed by an impaired driver; or to a nurse who sees babies born to drug-addicted mothers every day. It is well-known that crimes result from a variety of factors and often cannot be attributed solely to drug abuse. The connection between drug use and crime is difficult to quantify due to exaggeration or minimization by the offender, lack of prompt testing and inaccuracy of victims' descriptions of whether the offender used drugs. However, many of the criminal acts seen every day have their origins in drug use. The American public must be convinced of this.

> *The problem has been law enforcement's failure to effectively report its successes, warn of the true risks of substance abuse and to fully involve an educated community.*

The need to obtain money to feed a habit, the rage empowered by drugs, the protection or disruption of the drug marketplace—each has its role in the crime cycles surrounding drug use. There is an indisputable correlation between drug use and crime, and it is obvious that the combination of increased availability of drugs and a decrease in the stigma for drug use will result in an increase in crime. Although the number of drug-related homicides has decreased in recent years, murders related to narcotics rank as the fourth most documented murder circumstance of 24 possible categories. In 2000, the Uniform Crime Reporting Program of the FBI reported that 4.4 percent of the 12,943 homicides in which circumstances were known were narcotic-related. In 1998, 36 percent of convicted jail inmates were under the influence of drugs at the time of the offense. Drugs affect the user's judgment and behavior. In 1997, illicit drug users were 16 times more likely to be arrested for larceny or theft, 14 times more likely to be arrested for driving under the influence and more than nine times more likely to be arrested on assault charges.

During that same year, 29.4 percent of state and federal prison inmates reported being under the influence of drugs at the time they committed murder, 27.8 percent reported being under the influence of drugs at the time they committed robbery and 13.8 percent reported being under the influence at the time they committed assault. How much more proof is needed? Against these statistics, arguments that legalization will not impact crime rates do not hold up.

A final myth being advanced by legalization supporters is that decriminalization will not increase drug use. This is a fatalistic kind of a "que sera, sera" argument: "whatever will be, will be." Decriminalizing drugs sends the dangerous message that drug abuse is not harmful. This, an obvious lie, ignores the fact that drug abuse claims the lives of 14,000 Americans annually and costs taxpayers nearly $70 billion. In conveying this message, society would be tacitly approving the use of drugs. If drugs were legalized and market forces prevailed, what, for example, would stop the marijuana industry from sponsoring commercials for children to see during Super Bowl halftime?

According to the 2001 Monitoring the Future Study, 73.3 percent of high school seniors had used alcohol within the past 12 months. During the same period, 37 percent had used marijuana. Arguably, the difference is attributed to the fact that alcohol is more readily available because it is legal for adults to purchase and consume. Conversely, the private industrial sector has repeatedly demonstrated that a tough, enforced drug policy sharply reduces sick days, on-the-job accidents and workers' compensation claims. Drugs, even legally used, are not harmless; nor are they cost-free to society.

Drug War Successes

America's drug policy is not, as the critics contend, a dismal failure and a wasted effort. The statistics prove otherwise. The problem has been law enforcement's failure to effectively report its successes, warn of the true risks of substance abuse and to fully involve an educated community.

Overall drug use is down 50 percent since the late 1970s, which translates into 9.3 million fewer people using illegal drugs. Cocaine use has decreased 75 percent during the past 15 years, which means that 4 million fewer people are using cocaine on a règular basis. Less than 5 percent of the population use illegal drugs of any kind. Moreover, in the past, legalization and decriminalization reforms have failed, leading to increased drug use and the accompanying increases in social problems, health costs and economic repercussions. The use of drugs has decreased markedly since it reached the high point in the late 1970s, but it is not low enough. Too many Americans use drugs and too many other Americans are becoming victims of those who use drugs.

Even more dangerous is the complacency among prosecutors. If they, and others in law enforcement, do not sustain their efforts to tell the American people the truth about substance abuse, society as a whole will suffer and statistics on drug-related crime will continue to rise, fall and rise again as each generation relearns the mistakes of the previous generation. Law enforcement officers are sworn to protect the public and they need to be consistent and successful in their efforts to educate and warn society of the dangers of drug abuse. To date, there has not been success in these efforts. For the sake of the nation's future, success must be realized.

7

The War on Drugs Is Racist

Drug Policy Alliance

The Drug Policy Alliance is the leading organization work-ing to broaden the public debate on drug policy and to pro-mote alternatives to the war on drugs based on science, com-passion, health, and human rights.

The war on drugs has resulted in the imprisonment of more than half a million nonviolent drug offenders, 75 percent of whom are African Americans. It is obvious that the war on drugs is a war against minorities. This racist policy has destroyed lives, decimated communi-ties, and created a large underclass of ex-prisoners who are shut out of jobs, housing, and other economic op-portunities. Meanwhile, the war against illegal drugs has generated huge profits for major American corpora-tions that build prisons, use inmates to produce salable goods and provide profitable services, and otherwise ex-ploit prisoners in the "prison industrial complex." The United States must end the destructive war on drugs, tear down prisons, and make reparations to those whose lives have been shattered by the government's ill-conceived antidrug policies.

The U.S. war on drugs is big business—a multi-billion dollar public/private venture that radically inflates the value of il-legal drugs and criminalizes the poorest people of color, trap-ping them in a vicious cycle of addiction, unemployment and incarceration:

- $27 billion for interdiction and law enforcement, $1.3 bil-lion for Plan Colombia in 2000 [to stop drug production in Colombia].

- $9.4 billion in 2000 to imprison close to 500,000 people convicted of non-violent drug offenses, 75% of whom are Black.
- $80 to $100 billion in lost earnings.
- Untold billions in homeless shelters, healthcare, chemical dependency and psychiatric treatment, etc.

Black women are the fastest growing segment of the prison population and Native American prisoners are the largest group per capita. Approximately five million people—including those on probation and parole—are directly under the surveillance of the criminal justice system. The prison industrial complex profits from racist practices in arrest, conviction, and sentencing patterns. Black and brown bodies are the human raw material in a vast experiment to conceal the major social problems of our time.

The racially disproportionate demographics of the victims of the war on drugs will not surprise anyone familiar with the symbiotic relationship between poverty and institutionalized racism. Economic inequality and political disenfranchisement have been inextricably intertwined since the Trans-Atlantic slave trade. The racist enforcement of the drug laws is just the latest example of institutionalized racism.

As political economist John Flateau graphically puts it: "Metaphorically, the criminal justice pipeline is like a slave ship, transporting human cargo along interstate triangular trade routes from Black and Brown communities; through the middle passage of police precincts, holding pens, detention centers and courtrooms; to downstate jails or upstate prisons; back to communities as unrehabilitated escapees; and back to prison or jail in a vicious recidivist cycle."

Where Does the Money Go?

According to the United Nations International Drug Control Program, the international illicit drug business generates as much as $400 billion in trade annually. Profits of this magnitude invariably lead to corruption and complicity at the highest levels. Yet the so-called war on this illegal trade targets economically disadvantaged ethnic minorities and indigenous people in the U.S., Mexico, Colombia, Peru, Bolivia, Afghanistan, Pakistan, Myanmar, Laos, Thailand and Vietnam.

Putting aside the question of legality, there is no evidence of a "trickle-down effect." These substantial profits are not enriching the low level players who constitute the vast majority of drug offenders. To the contrary, the black market drug economy undermines non-drug-related businesses and limits the employability of its participants. . . .

Who Is Profiting?

In the United States, prison architects and contractors, corrections personnel, policymakers and academics, and the thousands of corporate vendors who peddle their wares at the annual trade-show of the American Corrections Association—hawking everything from toothbrushes and socks to barbed-wire fences and shackles. And multi-national corporations that win tax subsidies, incentives and abatements from local governments—robbing the public coffers and depriving communities of the kind of quality education, roads, health care and infrastructure that provide genuine incentives for legitimate business. The sale of tax-exempt bonds to underwrite prison construction is now estimated at $2.3 billion annually.

Black women are the fastest growing segment of the prison population and Native American prisoners are the largest group per capita.

Last year [2004], the Wackenhut Corrections Corporation—which manages or owns 37 prisons in the U.S., 18 in the U.K and Australia and has one under contract in South Africa—tried to convert a former slave plantation in North Carolina into a maximum security prison to warehouse mostly Black prisoners from the nation's capital. Promising investors to keep the prison cells filled, these corporations dispatch "bed-brokers" in search of prisoners—evoking images of 19th century bounty-hunters capturing runaway slaves and forcibly returning them to the cotton fields.

Corporations that appear to be far removed from the business of punishment are intimately involved in the expansion of the prison industrial complex. Prison construction bonds are one of the many sources of profitable investment for leading financiers such as Merrill Lynch. MCI charges prisoners and their families outrageous prices for the precious telephone calls which are often the only contact inmates have with the free world. Many corporations whose products we consume on a daily basis have learned that prison labor power can be as profitable as third world labor power exploited by U.S.-based global corporations. Both relegate formerly unionized workers to joblessness, many of which wind up in prison. Some of the companies that use prison labor are IBM, Motorola, Compaq, Texas Instruments, Honeywell, Microsoft, and Boeing. But it is not only the hi-tech industries that reap the profits of prison labor. Nordstrom department stores sell jeans that are marketed as "Prison Blues," as well as t-shirts and jackets made in Oregon prisons.

Racism and Poverty

Today there are over 2 million people incarcerated in the United States. Studies demonstrated that two-thirds of state prisoners had less than a high school education and 1/3 were unemployed at the time of arrest. Over the past decade states have financed prison construction at the expense of investment in higher education. At the same time, access to education in prison has been severely curtailed.

> *Many corporations whose products we consume on a daily basis have learned that prison labor power can be as profitable as third world labor power exploited by U.S.-based global corporations.*

Officially, 8.3% of working-age Blacks in the U.S. are unemployed but taking into account the "incarceration effect," the rate is significantly higher. Research confirms the obvious—the positive relationship between joblessness or low wages and recidivism. The stigma of prison has been codified in laws and licensing regulations that bar people with criminal records from countless jobs and opportunities, effectively excluding them from the legitimate workforce and forcing them into illegal ventures. As economists [Bruce] Western and [Becky] Petit point out, "[T]he penal system can be viewed as a type of labor market institution that systematically influence's men's employment . . . [and has a] pervasive influence . . . on the life chances of disadvantaged minorities."

Like slavery, the focused machinery of the war on drugs fractures families, as it destroys individual lives and destabilizes whole communities. It targets Native Americans living on or near reservations and urban minority neighborhoods, depressing incomes and repelling investment. "The lost potential earnings, savings, consumer demand, and human and social capital . . . cost black communities untold millions of dollars in potential economic development, worsening an inner-city political economy already crippled by decades of capital flight and de-industrialization [according to Western and Petit]."

The Case for Racial and Economic Justice

This reality is not the result of unintended consequence from otherwise well-reasoned policies. It is the logical, inevitable consequence of "tough-on-crime" laws and punitive sentencing polices that elected leaders and public officials embrace to avoid addressing the pressing social problems caused by institutionalized racism and political and economic exclusion.

By incarcerating high proportions of low-income Black, Latino and Native American residents and maintaining surveillance over them for even longer periods of time, the "war on drugs" and its criminal justice apparatus perpetuate a social segregation policy that intentionally isolates historically disadvantaged racial and ethnic minorities and communities, ensuring a capital divestment policy that builds neither social capital nor economic infrastructure.

According to the United States Department of State's 2000 report to the United Nations Commission on the Elimination of Racial Discrimination (CERD), "discrimination in the criminal justice system" is a "principal causative factor" hindering progress toward ending racial discrimination in [U.S.] society. If the United States takes seriously its mandates of equality and peace with justice, then the war on drugs and the prison industrial complex must be dismantled and reparation made for the devastation they have wrought. Decimated communities must be rebuilt and enriched and barriers torn down in order to guarantee Blacks and other ethnic minorities a fair playing field. Only then can the United States begin to acknowledge responsibility for the damning impact of slavery and its perpetuation through the institutionalization of racism and poverty.

8

Marijuana Prohibition Is Misguided

Ethan A. Nadelmann

Ethan A. Nadelmann is the founder and executive director of the Drug Policy Alliance, an organization that promotes alternatives to the drug war.

While marijuana is one of the least addictive and most benign drugs, the federal government continues to classify it as one of the most dangerous, putting it in the same legal category as crack cocaine, LSD, and heroin. This policy prompts local and federal authorities to arrest more than seven hundred thousand people a year for marijuana sales and possession. Police resources could be better used to fight truly dangerous drugs. Instead, the government is waging a misguided and failed war on a harmless drug that has been smoked by people for thousands of years.

Never before have so many Americans supported decriminalizing and even legalizing marijuana. Seventy-two percent say that for simple marijuana possession, people should not be incarcerated but fined: the generally accepted definition of "decriminalization." Even more Americans support making marijuana legal for medical purposes. Support for broader legalization ranges between 25 and 42 percent, depending on how one asks the question. Two of every five Americans—according to a 2003 Zogby poll—say "the government should treat marijuana more or less the same way it treats alcohol: It should regulate it, control it, tax it, and only make it illegal for children."

Ethan A. Nadelmann, "An End to Marijuana Prohibition," *National Review*, July 12, 2004. Copyright © 2004 by the National Review, Inc., 215 Lexington Ave., New York, NY 10016. Reproduced by permission.

Close to 100 million Americans—including more than half of those between the ages of 18 and 50—have tried marijuana at least once. Military and police recruiters often have no choice but to ignore past marijuana use by job seekers. The public apparently feels the same way about presidential and other political candidates. Al Gore, Bill Bradley, and John Kerry all say they smoked pot in days past. So did Bill Clinton, with his notorious caveat [saying "I didn't inhale"]. George W. Bush won't deny he did. And ever more political, business, religious, intellectual, and other leaders plead guilty as well.

The debate over ending marijuana prohibition simmers just below the surface of mainstream politics, crossing ideological and partisan boundaries. Marijuana is no longer the symbol of Sixties rebellion and Seventies permissiveness, and it's not just liberals and libertarians who say it should be legal, as [conservative commentator] William F. Buckley Jr. has demonstrated better than anyone. As director of the country's leading drug policy reform organization, I've had countless conversations with police and prosecutors, judges and politicians, and hundreds of others who quietly agree that the criminalization of marijuana is costly, foolish, and destructive. What's most needed now is principled conservative leadership. Buckley has led the way, and New Mexico's former governor, Gary Johnson, spoke out courageously while in office. How about others?

Overreaction

Marijuana prohibition is unique among American criminal laws. No other law is both enforced so widely and harshly and yet deemed unnecessary by such a substantial portion of the populace.

Police make about 700,000 arrests per year for marijuana offenses. That's almost the same number as are arrested each year for cocaine, heroin, methamphetamine, Ecstasy, and all other illicit drugs combined. Roughly 600,000 or 87 percent, of marijuana arrests are for nothing more than possession of small amounts. Millions of Americans have never been arrested or convicted of any criminal offense except this. Enforcing marijuana laws costs an estimated $10–15 billion in direct costs alone.

Punishments range widely across the country, from modest fines to a few days in jail to many years in prison. Prosecutors often contend that no one goes to prison for simple possession—but tens, perhaps hundreds, of thousands of people on probation and parole are locked up each year because their urine tested positive for marijuana or because they were picked up in possession of a joint. Alabama currently locks up people convicted three times of marijuana *possession* for 15 years to life. There are probably—no firm estimates exist—100,000 Americans behind bars tonight for one marijuana offense or another. And even for those who don't lose their freedom, simply being arrested can be traumatic and costly. A parent's marijuana use can be the basis for taking away her children and putting them in foster care. Foreign-born residents of the U.S. can be deported for a marijuana offense no matter how long they have lived in this country, no matter if their children are U.S. citizens, and no matter how long they have been legally employed. More than half the states revoke or suspend driver's licenses of people arrested for marijuana possession even though they were not driving at the time of arrest. The federal Higher Education Act prohibits student loans to young people convicted of any drug offense; all other criminal offenders remain eligible.

This is clearly an overreaction on the part of government. No drug is perfectly safe, and every psychoactive drug can be used in ways that are problematic. The federal government has spent billions of dollars on advertisements and anti-drug programs that preach the dangers of marijuana—that it's a gateway drug, and addictive in its own right, and dramatically more potent that it used to be, and responsible for all sorts of physical and social diseases as well as international terrorism. But the government has yet to repudiate the 1988 finding of the Drug Enforcement Administration's [DEA] own administrative law judge, Francis Young, who concluded after extensive testimony that "marijuana in its natural form is one of the safest therapeutically active substances known to man."

Drug War Myths

Is marijuana a gateway drug? Yes, insofar as most Americans try marijuana before they try other illicit drugs. But no, insofar as the vast majority of Americans who have tried marijuana have never gone on to try other illegal drugs, much less get in trouble with them, and most have never even gone on to become regular or problem marijuana users. Trying to reduce heroin addiction by preventing marijuana use, it's been said, is like trying to reduce motorcycle fatalities by cracking down on bicycle riding. If marijuana did not exist, there's little reason to believe that there would be less drug abuse in the U.S.; indeed, its role would most likely be filled by a more dangerous substance.

Is marijuana dramatically more potent today? There's certainly a greater variety of high-quality marijuana available today than 30 years ago. But anyone who smoked marijuana in the 1970s and 1980s can recall smoking pot that was just as strong as anything available today. What's more, one needs to take only a few puffs of higher-potency pot to get the desired effect, so there's less wear and tear on the lungs.

> *No other law is both enforced so widely and harshly and yet deemed unnecessary by such a substantial portion of the populace.*

Is marijuana addictive? Yes, it can be, in that some people use it to excess, in ways that are problematic for themselves and those around them, and find it hard to stop. But marijuana may well be the least addictive and least damaging of all commonly used psychoactive drugs, including many that are now legal. Most people who smoke marijuana never become dependent. Withdrawal symptoms pale compared with those from other drugs. No one has ever died from a marijuana overdose, which cannot be said of most other drugs. Marijuana is not associated with violent behavior and only minimally with reckless sexual behavior. And even heavy marijuana smokers smoke only a fraction of what cigarette addicts smoke. Lung cancers involving only marijuana are rare.

The government's most recent claim is that marijuana abuse accounts for more people entering treatment than any other illegal drug. That shouldn't be surprising, given that tens of millions of Americans smoke marijuana while only a few million use all other illicit drugs. But the claim is spurious nonetheless. Few Americans who enter "treatment" for marijuana are addicted. Fewer than one in five people entering drug treatment for marijuana do so voluntarily. More than half were referred by the criminal justice system. They go because they got caught with a joint or failed a drug test at school or work (typically for having smoked marijuana days ago, not for being impaired), or because they were caught by a law-enforcement officer—and attending a marijuana "treatment" program is what's required to avoid expulsion, dismissal, or incarceration. Many traditional drug treatment programs shamelessly participate in this charade to preserve a profitable and captive client stream.

Even those who recoil at the "nanny state" telling adults what they can or cannot sell to one another often make an exception when it comes to marijuana—to "protect the kids." This is a bad joke, as any teenager will attest. The criminalization of marijuana for adults has not prevented young people from having better access to marijuana than anyone else. Even as marijuana's popularity has waxed and waned since the 1970s, one statistic has remained constant: More than 80 percent of high school students report it's easy to get. Meanwhile, the government's exaggerations and outright dishonesty easily backfire. For every teen who refrains from trying marijuana because it's illegal (for adults), another is tempted by its status as "forbidden fruit." Many respond to the lies about marijuana by disbelieving warnings about more dangerous drugs. So much for protecting the kids by criminalizing the adults.

The Medical Dimension

The debate over medical marijuana obviously colors the broader debate over marijuana prohibition. Marijuana's medical efficacy is no longer in serious dispute. Its use as a medicine dates back thousands of years. Pharmaceutical products containing marijuana's central ingredient, THC, are legally sold in the U.S. and more are emerging. Some people find the pill form satisfactory, and others consume it in teas or baked products. Most find smoking the easiest and most effective way to consume this unusual medicine, but non-smoking consumption methods, notably vaporizers, are emerging.

> *The federal Higher Education Act prohibits student loans to young people convicted of any drug offense; all other criminal offenders remain eligible.*

Federal law still prohibits medical marijuana. But every state ballot initiative to legalize medical marijuana has been approved, often by wide margins—in California, Washington,

Oregon, Alaska, Colorado, Nevada, Maine, and Washington, D.C. State legislatures in Vermont, Hawaii, and Maryland have followed suit. . . . Support is often bipartisan, with Republican governors like Gary Johnson and Maryland's Bob Ehrlich taking the lead. In New York's 2002 gubernatorial campaign, the conservative candidate of the Independence party, Tom Golisano, surprised everyone by campaigning heavily on this issue. The medical marijuana bill before the New York legislature [in July 2004] is backed not just by leading Republicans but even by some Conservative party leaders.

> *Marijuana may well be the least addictive and least damaging of all commonly used psychoactive drugs, including many that are now legal.*

The political battleground increasingly pits the White House —first under Clinton and now Bush—against everyone else. Majorities in virtually every state in the country would vote, if given the chance, to legalize medical marijuana. Even Congress is beginning to turn; [in 2003] about two-thirds of House Democrats and a dozen Republicans voted in favor of an amendment co-sponsored by Republican Dana Rohrabacher to prohibit federal funding of any Justice Department crackdowns on medical marijuana in the states that had legalized it. (Many more Republicans privately expressed support, but were directed to vote against.) And federal courts have imposed limits on federal aggression: first in *Conant v. Walters*, which now protects the First Amendment rights of doctors and patients to discuss medical marijuana, and more recently in *Raich v. Ashcroft* and *Santa Cruz v. Ashcroft*, which determined that the federal government's power to regulate interstate commerce does not provide a basis for prohibiting medical marijuana operations that are entirely local and non-commercial. (The Supreme Court let the *Conant* decision stand, but has yet to consider the others.)

State and local governments are increasingly involved in trying to regulate medical marijuana, notwithstanding the federal prohibition. California, Oregon, Hawaii, Alaska, Colorado, and Nevada have created confidential medical marijuana patient registries, which protect bona fide patients and caregivers from arrest or prosecution. Some municipal governments are now trying to figure out how to regulate production and distribution. In California, where dozens of medical marijuana programs now operate openly, with tacit approval by local authorities, some program directors are asking to be licensed and regulated. Many state and local authorities, including law enforcement, favor this but are intimidated by federal threats to arrest and prosecute them for violating federal law.

> // State and local governments are increasingly involved in trying to regulate medical marijuana, notwithstanding the federal prohibition. //

The drug czar [John Walters, head of the Office of National Drug Control Policy] and DEA spokespersons recite the mantra that "there is no such thing as medical marijuana," but the claim is so specious on its face that it clearly undermines federal credibility. The federal government currently provides marijuana—from its own production site in Mississippi—to a few patients who years ago were recognized by the courts as bona fide patients. No one wants to debate those who have used marijuana for medical purposes, be it Santa Cruz medical-marijuana hospice founder Valerie Corral or *National Review's* Richard Brookhiser. Even many federal officials quietly regret the assault on medical marijuana. When the DEA raided Corral's hospice in September 2002, one agent was heard to say, "Maybe I'm going to think about getting another job sometime soon."

The Broader Movement

The bigger battle, of course, concerns whether marijuana prohibition will ultimately go the way of alcohol Prohibition, replaced by a variety of state and local tax and regulatory policies with modest federal involvement. Dedicated prohibitionists see medical marijuana as the first step down a slippery slope to full legalization. The voters who approved the medical-marijuana ballot initiatives (as well as the wealthy men who helped fund the campaigns) were roughly divided between those who support broader legalization and those who don't, but united in seeing the criminalization and persecution of medical marijuana patients as the most distasteful aspect of the war on marijuana. (This was a point that Buckley made forcefully in his columns about the plight of Peter McWilliams, who likely died because federal authorities effectively forbade him to use marijuana as medicine.)

The medical marijuana effort has probably aided the broader anti-prohibitionist campaign in three ways. It helped transform the face of marijuana in the media, from the stereotypical rebel with long hair and tie-dyed shirt to an ordinary middle-aged American struggling with MS or cancer or AIDS. By winning first Proposition 215, the 1996 medical-marijuana ballot initiative in California, and then a string of similar victories in other states, the nascent drug policy reform movement demonstrated that it could win in the big leagues of American politics. And the emergence of successful models of medical marijuana control is likely to boost public confidence in the possibilities and virtue of regulating nonmedical use as well.

> *If the emerging system is successful in controlling production and distribution of marijuana for those with a medical need, can it not also expand to provide for those without medical need?*

In this regard, the history of Dutch policy on cannabis (i.e., marijuana and hashish) is instructive. The "coffee shop" model in the Netherlands, where retail (but not wholesale) sale of cannabis is de facto legal, was not legislated into existence. It evolved in fits and starts following the decriminalization of cannabis by Parliament in 1976, as consumers, growers, and entrepreneurs negotiated and collaborated with local police, prosecutors, and other authorities to find an acceptable middle-ground policy. "Coffee shops" now operate throughout the country, subject to local regulations. Troublesome shops are shut down, and most are well integrated into local city cultures. Cannabis is no more popular than in the U.S. and other Western countries, notwithstanding the effective absence of criminal sanctions and controls. Parallel developments are now underway in other countries.

Like the Dutch decriminalization law in 1976, California's Prop 215 in 1996 initiated a dialogue over how best to implement the new law. The variety of outlets that have emerged—ranging from pharmacy-like stores to medical "coffee shops" to hospices, all of which provide marijuana only to people with a patient ID card or doctor's recommendations—play a key role as the most public symbol and manifestation of this dialogue. More such outlets will likely pop up around the country as other states legalize marijuana for medical purposes and then seek ways to regulate distribution and access. And the question will inevitably arise: If the emerging system is successful in controlling production and distribution of marijuana for those with a medical need, can it not also expand to provide for those without medical need?

Millions of Americans use marijuana not just "for fun" but because they find it useful for many of the same reasons that people drink alcohol or take pharmaceutical drugs. It's akin to the beer, glass of wine, or cocktail at the end of the workday, or the prescribed drug to alleviate depression or anxiety, or the sleeping pill, or the aid to sexual function and pleasure. More and more Americans are apt to describe some or all of their marijuana use as "medical" as the definition of that term evolves and broadens. Their anecdotal experiences are increasingly backed by new scientific research into marijuana's essential ingredients, the cannabinoids. [In 2003], a subsidiary of *The Lancet*, Britain's leading medical journal, speculated whether marijuana might soon emerge as the "aspirin of the 21st century," providing a wide array of medical benefits at low cost to diverse populations.

Perhaps the expansion of the medical-control model provides the best answer—at least in the U.S.—to the question of how best to reduce the substantial costs and harms of marijuana prohibition without inviting significant increases in real drug abuse. It's analogous to the evolution of many pharmaceutical drugs from prescription to over-the-counter, but with stricter controls still in place. It's also an incrementalist approach to reform that can provide both the control and reassurance that cautious politicians and voters desire.

9

Legalizing Marijuana Would Harm Teens

Robert Margolis

Robert Margolis is a licensed clinical psychologist who has specialized in adolescent addiction and substance abuse. He is the director of the Solutions Intensive Outpatient Program, a treatment program for adolescents in Roswell, Georgia.

While legalization advocates claim that marijuana is harmless, studies show that millions of people have had problems with the drug. Heavy users of marijuana develop dependency while exposing themselves to carcinogens present in the smoke. Worse, studies show that teens who smoke pot are much more likely to experience problems at home, in school, and on the job. While pot promoters say marijuana should be available to adults only, there is little doubt that the drug will fall into the hands of teenagers just as many obtain alcohol and cigarettes today. A drug like marijuana is too dangerous to legalize and such a social experiment would have a negative effect on teenagers. Vulnerable young people do not need another problem added to the many they already face in modern society.

We are in the midst of a major national debate on the legalization of marijuana. The outcome of this debate is likely to have profound implications for our society. To make an informed choice on this issue, we need accurate information about these implications.

There has never been a greater need for unbiased scientific data on the physical and psychological effects of marijuana use. Unfortunately, there has been more heat than light shed on this issue in the mainstream media.

Perhaps with this in mind, the National Institute on Drug Abuse [NIDA] has just issued a major research report on the effects of marijuana. The report may be surprising to most people who regard marijuana as a benign or harmless drug.

According to NIDA, marijuana is a drug that can and does cause addiction. THC, the active ingredient in marijuana, activates the brain's reward system in the same way as other drugs of abuse—by triggering the release of dopamine.

> *Rats treated with THC showed nerve cell loss resulting in memory loss.*

Dopamine, a chemical found in the brain, is associated with a sense of euphoria. Like other drugs of abuse, chronic administration of marijuana depletes dopamine supplies and causes other brain changes, which creates a craving for the drug. After a certain period of time, cessation of use results in a defined marijuana withdrawal syndrome as demonstrated in both animal and human studies. These factors combined with other functional impairments define drug dependence or addiction. According to NIDA, more than 2 million people met the criteria for marijuana dependence in 1999 alone.

Major Problems

Marijuana also causes major problems with learning, memory, concentration and judgment. Individuals who smoke marijuana have an impaired ability to learn for at least 24 hours. Long-term users have been shown to be impaired for up to four weeks after cessation of use. In animal studies, rats treated with THC showed nerve cell loss resulting in memory loss. The nerve cell loss was "equivalent to that of unexposed animals twice their age," according to the report.

Marijuana also contains more carcinogenic material than cigarettes and has been statistically linked to cancer. It also impairs the immune system's ability to fight off diseases and infections. It increases the risk of a heart attack fourfold for the first hour after smoking it. Students who smoke marijuana get lower grades and are less likely to graduate from high school than their nonsmoking peers. Workers who smoke marijuana experience a variety of problems, absences, tardiness, accidents, etc., when compared with workers who do not smoke marijuana.

The fact that marijuana is a dangerous, addictive drug is not in and of itself a definitive reason for it to be illegal. Alcohol is certainly a dangerous, addictive drug that is legal. It is, however, a reason to have a careful, reasoned debate before we make decisions about legalization.

Some hard questions need to be asked. How does this affect productivity in society? How will the health of individuals be affected? Perhaps, most importantly, what impact will legalization have on our children?

As someone who has worked for more than 20 years with teenagers who smoke marijuana, I am aware that it becomes difficult to tell kids not to smoke marijuana when society is actively moving toward legalization. These questions deserve more debate and discussion before we move forward with a decision that can have powerful negative implications and may be almost impossible to undo.

10

Medical Marijuana Should Be Legalized

Marijuana Policy Project

The Marijuana Policy Project (MPP) works to minimize the harm associated with marijuana—both the consumption of marijuana, and the laws that are intended to prohibit such use. MPP believes that the greatest harm associated with marijuana is prison. To this end, MPP focuses on removing criminal penalties for marijuana use, with a particular emphasis on making marijuana medically available to seriously ill people whose doctors have approved their use of the drug.

Marijuana has many medical benefits, including the relief from nausea, reduction of muscle spasms, and relief from chronic pain. However, the 1937 Marijuana Tax Act federally prohibited the smoking of marijuana for any purpose. In addition, the Controlled Substance Act of 1970 placed all drugs into five categories depending on their utility as medicine and perceived harm; marijuana was placed in Schedule I, defining it as having a high potential for abuse and no medicinal qualities. Nevertheless, illicit marijuana use continued, with many people realizing the therapeutic qualities of the drug. Several states legalized medical marijuana, but since federal law still prohibits its use users in those states are subject to arrest. This situation is untenable. The federal government should legalize marijuana so that patients sick with cancer, AIDS, and other illnesses can reap the enormous benefits of smoking the drug.

Marijuana Policy Project, "Medical Marijuana Briefing Paper–2003: The Need to Change State and Federal Law," www.mpp.org, 2003.

For thousands of years, marijuana has been used to treat a wide variety of ailments. Until 1937, marijuana (*Cannabis sativa L.*) was legal in the United States for all purposes. Presently, federal law allows only seven Americans to use marijuana as a medicine.

On March 17, 1999, the National Academy of Sciences' Institute of Medicine (IOM) concluded that "there are some limited circumstances in which we recommend smoking marijuana for medical uses." The IOM report, the result of two years of research that was funded by the White House drug policy office, analyzed all existing data on marijuana's therapeutic uses. Please see http://www.mpp.org/science.html.

Medicinal Value

Marijuana is one of the safest therapeutically active substances known. No one has ever died from an overdose, and it has a wide variety of therapeutic applications, including:

- Relief from nausea and appetite loss;
- Reduction of intraocular (within the eye) pressure;
- Reduction of muscle spasms; and
- Relief from chronic pain.

> *Marijuana is one of the safest therapeutically active substances known.*

Marijuana is frequently beneficial in the treatment of the following conditions:

AIDS. Marijuana can reduce the nausea, vomiting, and loss of appetite caused by the ailment itself and by various AIDS medications.

Glaucoma. Marijuana can reduce intraocular pressure, alleviating the pain and slowing—and sometimes stopping—damage to the eyes. (Glaucoma is the leading cause of blindness in the United States. It damages vision by increasing eye pressure over time.)

Cancer. Marijuana can stimulate the appetite and alleviate nausea and vomiting, which are side effects of chemotherapy treatment.

Multiple Sclerosis. Marijuana can limit the muscle pain and spasticity caused by the disease, as well as relieving tremor and unsteadiness of gait. (Multiple sclerosis is the leading cause of neurological disability among young and middle-aged adults in the United States.)

Epilepsy. Marijuana can prevent epileptic seizures in some patients.

Chronic Pain. Marijuana can alleviate the chronic, often debilitating pain caused by myriad disorders and injuries.

Each of these applications has been deemed legitimate by at least one court, legislature, and/or government agency in the United States.

Many patients also report that marijuana is useful for treating arthritis, migraine, menstrual cramps, alcohol and opiate addiction, and depression and other debilitating mood disorders.

Marijuana could be helpful for millions of patients in the United States. Nevertheless, other than for the seven people with special permission from the federal government, medical marijuana remains illegal under federal law!

People currently suffering from any of the conditions mentioned above, for whom the legal medical options have proven unsafe or ineffective, have two options:

1. Continue to suffer without effective treatment; or
2. Illegally obtain marijuana—and risk suffering consequences directly related to its illegality, such as:
   - an insufficient supply due to the prohibition-inflated price or scarcity;
   - impure, contaminated, or chemically adulterated marijuana;
   - arrests, fines, court costs, property forfeiture, incarceration, probation, and criminal records.

Background

Prior to 1937, at least 27 medicines containing marijuana were legally available in the United States. Many were made by well-known pharmaceutical firms that still exist today, such as Squibb (now Bristol-Myers Squibb) and Eli Lilly. The Marijuana Tax Act of 1937 federally prohibited marijuana. Dr. William C. Woodward of the American Medical Association opposed the Act, testifying that prohibition would ultimately prevent the medicinal uses of marijuana.

The Controlled Substances Act of 1970 placed all illicit and prescription drugs into five "schedules" (categories). *Marijuana was placed in Schedule I, defining it as having a high potential for abuse, no currently accepted medical use in treatment in the United States, and a lack of accepted safety for use under medical supervision.*

This definition simply does not apply to marijuana. Of course, at the time of the Controlled Substances Act, marijuana had been prohibited for more than three decades. Its medicinal uses forgotten, marijuana was considered a dangerous and addictive narcotic.

> *A substantial increase in the number of recreational users in the 1970s contributed to the rediscovery of marijuana's medicinal uses.*

A substantial increase in the number of recreational users in the 1970s contributed to the rediscovery of marijuana's medicinal uses:

- Many scientists studied the health effects of marijuana and inadvertently discovered marijuana's medicinal uses in the process.
- Many who used marijuana recreationally also suffered from diseases for which marijuana is beneficial. By accident, they discovered its therapeutic value.

As the word spread, more and more patients started self-medicating with marijuana. However, marijuana's Schedule I status bars doctors from prescribing it and severely curtails research.

The Struggle in Court

In 1972, a petition was submitted to the Bureau of Narcotics and Dangerous Drugs—now the Drug Enforcement Administration (DEA)—to reschedule marijuana to make it available by prescription.

After 16 years of court battles, the DEA's chief administrative law judge, Francis L. Young, ruled:

"Marijuana, in its natural form, is one of the safest therapeutically active substances known. . . .

". . . [T]he provisions of the [Controlled Substances] Act permit and require the transfer of marijuana from Schedule I to Schedule II.

"It would be unreasonable, arbitrary and capricious for DEA

to continue to stand between those sufferers and the benefits of this substance. . . ."

(September 6, 1988)

Marijuana's placement in Schedule II would enable doctors to prescribe it to their patients. But top DEA bureaucrats rejected Judge Young's ruling and refused to reschedule marijuana. Two appeals later, petitioners experienced their first defeat in the 22-year-old lawsuit. On February 18, 1994, the U.S. Court of Appeals (D.C. Circuit) ruled that the DEA is allowed to reject its judge's ruling and set its own criteria—enabling the DEA to keep marijuana in Schedule I.

However, Congress has the power to reschedule marijuana via legislation, regardless of the DEA's wishes.

Temporary Compassion

In 1975, Robert Randall, who suffered from glaucoma, was arrested for cultivating his own marijuana. He won his case by using the "medical necessity defense," forcing the government to find a way to provide him with his medicine. As a result, the Investigational New Drug (IND) compassionate access program was established, enabling some patients to receive marijuana from the government.

> *There is wide support for ending the prohibition of medical marijuana.*

The program was grossly inadequate at helping the potentially millions of people who need medical marijuana. Many patients would never consider the idea that an illegal drug might be their best medicine, and most who were fortunate enough to discover marijuana's medicinal value did not discover the IND program. Those who did often could not find doctors willing to take on the program's arduous, bureaucratic requirements.

In 1992, in response to a flood of new applications from AIDS patients, the George H.W. Bush administration closed the program to new applicants, and pleas to reopen it were ignored by subsequent administrations. The IND program remains in operation only for the seven surviving, previously-approved patients.

Public and Professional Opinion

There is wide support for ending the prohibition of medical marijuana among both the public and the medical community:

• Since 1996, a majority of voters in Alaska, California, Colorado, the District of Columbia, Maine, Montana, Nevada, Oregon, and Washington state have voted in favor of ballot initiatives to remove criminal penalties for seriously ill people who grow or possess medical marijuana. Polls have shown that public approval of these laws has increased since they went into effect.

• A CNN/*Time* poll published November 4, 2002 found that 80% of Americans believe that "adults should be allowed to legally use marijuana for medical purposes if their doctor prescribes it. . . ." Over the last decade, polls have consistently shown between 60% and 80% support for legal access to medical marijuana. Both a statewide Alabama poll commissioned by the *Mobile Register*, published in July 2004, and a November 2004 Scripps Howard Texas poll reported 75% support.

> *Congress has the power and the responsibility to change federal law so that seriously ill people nationwide can use medical marijuana.*

• Organizations supporting some form of physician-supervised access to medical marijuana include the American Academy of Family Physicians, American Nurses Association, American Public Health Association, the *New England Journal of Medicine* and many others.

• A 1990 scientific survey of oncologists (cancer specialists) found that 54% of those with an opinion favored the controlled medical availability of marijuana and 44% had already suggested at least once that a patient obtain marijuana illegally. [R. Doblin & M. Kleiman, "Marijuana as Antiemetic Medicine," *Journal of Clinical Oncology* 9 (1991): 1314–1319.]

Changing State Laws

The federal government has no legal authority to prevent state governments from changing their laws to remove state-level criminal penalties for medical marijuana use. Hawaii enacted a medical marijuana law via its state legislature in 2000 and Vermont enacted a similar law in 2004. State legislatures have the authority and moral responsibility to change state law to:

- exempt seriously ill patients from state-level prosecution for medical marijuana possession and cultivation; and
- exempt doctors who recommend medical marijuana from prosecution or the denial of any right or privilege.

Even within the confines of federal law, states can enact reforms that have the practical effect of removing the fear of patients being arrested and prosecuted under state law—as well as the symbolic effect of pushing the federal government to allow doctors to prescribe marijuana.

U.S. Congress: The Final Battleground

State governments that want to allow marijuana to be sold in pharmacies have been stymied by the federal government's overriding prohibition of marijuana.

Patients' efforts to bring change through the federal courts have made little progress, as the courts tend to defer to the DEA, which works aggresively to keep marijuana illegal. However, a Supreme Court case being considered during the 2004–2005 session could limit federal attacks on patients in states with medical marijuana laws.

Efforts to obtain FDA approval of marijuana are similarly stalled. Though some small studies of marijuana are now underway, the National Institute on Drug Abuse—the only legal source of marijuana for clinical research in the U.S.—has consistently made it difficult (and often nearly impossible) for researchers to obtain marijuana for their studies. At present, it is effectively impossible to do the sort of large-scale, extremely costly trials required for FDA approval.

In the meantime, patients continue to suffer. *Congress has the power and the responsibility to change federal law so that seriously ill people nationwide can use medical marijuana without fear of arrest and imprisonment.*

11

Medical Marijuana Should Remain Illegal

David G. Evans and John E. Lamp

David G. Evans and John E. Lamp are lawyers.

Marijuana should not be legalized for medicinal purposes. Marijuana smoke contains known carcinogens and produces dependency in heavy users. In addition, medical marijuana causes intoxication in patients and should not under any circumstances be smoked before driving or operating dangerous machinery. While pot promoters claim that marijuana is the only drug that can alleviate suffering from cancer, AIDS, glaucoma, and other conditions, there are many pharmaceutical drugs that have been approved to help patients with those illnesses. The problems and dangers associated with marijuana are too great for the government to classify this drug as a Schedule II substance, which deems it useful as medicine. Marijuana must remain a Schedule I drug, meaning it is highly addictive and lacking any medicinal value.

Editor's note: The following article is excerpted from a "friend of the court" legal brief, written by lawyers working for several anti-drug groups, such as the Drug Free America Foundation. Although these groups were interested in the outcome, they were not directly involved in the 2001 medical marijuana case before the Ninth Circuit Court of Appeals, the United States v. Oakland Cannabis Buyers' Cooperative (OCBC). *The OCBC is a group that provided medical marijuana to patients with a variety of diseases. The case is still under consideration.*

David G. Evans and John E. Lamp, "Amicus Curiae Brief: *United States v. Oakland Cannabis Buyers' Cooperative,*" www.nationalfamilies.org, National Families in Action, 2001.

Throughout this brief we use the term "crude marijuana" to describe the illicit Schedule I drug that people abuse. The drug is derived from the leaves and flowering tops of the Cannabis plant and is consumed in a variety of ways. . . .

There is a strong governmental interest in prohibiting the distribution of crude marijuana as medicine. The federal government strives to protect our citizens from unsafe, ineffective substances sold as "medicines" and from drug abuse, drug addiction, and the abusive and criminal behaviors that marijuana and other illicit drugs often generate. The OCBC [Oakland Cannabis Buyers' Cooperative] is distributing an unproven drug in disregard of the government's objective to ensure the safety and efficacy of medicines. . . .

[In order for marijuana to be sold as "medicine"] the drug must first be approved by the Food and Drug Administration (the "FDA"). The federal Food, Drug, and Cosmetics Act, gives the federal government sole responsibility for determining that drugs are safe and effective, a requirement all medicines must meet before they may be distributed to the public. The FDA has not approved marijuana as safe or effective, so the drug may not legally be prescribed and sold as a medicine.

Not only has the FDA failed to approve marijuana, but marijuana is a Schedule I controlled substance under the Controlled Substances Act. Schedule I drugs have "1) a high potential for abuse, 2) no currently accepted treatment in the United States, and 3) a lack of accepted safety for use of the drug . . . under medical supervision."

In [the court case] *Alliance for Cannabis Therapeutics v. DEA*, the United States District Court for the District of Columbia accepted the Drug Enforcement Administration's new five-part test for determining whether a drug is in "currently accepted medical use." The test requires that:

1. The drug's chemistry must be known and reproducible;
2. there must be adequate safety studies;
3. there must be adequate and well-controlled studies proving efficacy;
4. the drug must be accepted by qualified experts; and
5. the scientific evidence must be widely available.

Applying these criteria to a petition to reschedule crude marijuana [to a Schedule II drug that would allow it to be used as medicine], the court found that the drug had no currently accepted medical use and, therefore, had to remain in Schedule I. Thus, the OCBC disregarded the FDA's statutorily prescribed mandate created to ensure drug safety and is distributing an untested, unsafe Schedule I drug in violation of the Controlled Substances Act. . . .

No Future as Medicine

Crude marijuana is derived from the leaves and flowering tops of the Cannabis plant. It contains some 400 chemicals, most of which have not been studied by scientists. Some 60 of these chemicals, called cannabinoids, are unique to the Cannabis plant. One cannabinoid, Delta-9-tetrahydrocannabinol (THC), was synthesized, tested, and approved by [the] FDA in 1985 for treating nausea in cancer patients and wasting in AIDS patients. The drug's generic name is dronabinol and its trade name is Marinol®. It is produced by Unimed Pharmaceuticals.

> *While we see a future in the development of chemically defined cannabinoid drugs, we see little future in smoked marijuana as a medicine.*

According to John Benson, Jr., M.D., of the Institute of Medicine, research on other cannabinoids is underway and some of these chemicals may one day prove to be useful medicines. However, he states:

> While we see a future in the development of chemically defined cannabinoid drugs, we see little future in smoked marijuana as a medicine.

The fact that crude marijuana contains a chemical that has been synthesized, tested, and approved for medical use does not make marijuana itself a safe or effective medicine. Modern pharmaceutical science would require all the 400 or more chemicals in marijuana to pass the safety and efficacy tests in research, and this has not happened. Any consideration of this issue must take into account the substantial toxicity and morbidity associated with marijuana use. Because of the impurity of crude marijuana and its known toxic effects, it does not represent a useful medical alternative to currently available medications. Furthermore, efforts to gain legal status of marijuana through ballot initiatives seriously threaten the Food and Drug

Administration process of proving safety and efficacy, and they create an atmosphere of medicine by popular vote, rather than the rigorous scientific and medical process that all medicines must undergo.

Before the development of modern pharmaceutical science, the field of medicine was fraught with potions and herbal remedies. Many of those were absolutely useless, or conversely were harmful to unsuspecting subjects. Thus evolved our current Food and Drug Administration and drug scheduling processes, which should not be undermined.

Having extensively reviewed available therapies for chemotherapy-associated nausea, glaucoma, multiple sclerosis, and appetite stimulation, Drs. [E.A.] Voth and [R.A.] Schwartz have determined that no compelling need exists to make crude marijuana available as a medicine for physicians to prescribe. They concluded that the most appropriate direction for THC research is to research specific cannabinoids or synthetic analogs rather than pursuing the smoking of marijuana.

> *Neither smoked marijuana nor cannabinoids are as effective as current medicines that stop nausea and vomiting in cancer chemotherapy patients.*

The conclusions Drs. Voth and Schwartz were echoed a year later by the National Academy of Science's Institute of Medicine (hereinafter "IOM Report") in an assessment of scientific marijuana and cannabinoid research.

Available research on the utility of THC has demonstrated some effectiveness of the purified form of the drug in treating nausea associated with cancer chemotherapy. . . .

Legalization advocates would have the public and policy makers incorrectly believe that crude marijuana is the only treatment alternative for masses of cancer sufferers who are going untreated for the nausea associated with chemotherapy, and for all those who suffer from glaucoma, multiple sclerosis, and other ailments. Numerous effective medications are, however, currently available for conditions such as nausea.

In fact, The IOM report found that neither smoked marijuana nor cannabinoids are as effective as current medicines

that stop nausea and vomiting in cancer chemotherapy patients. However, the scientists speculated that cannabinoids
might be effective in those few patients who respond poorly to
current antiemetic (anti-nausea) drugs or more effective in combination with current antiemetics. It recommended that research should be pursued for patients who do not respond completely to current antiemetics and that a safe (non-smoking)
delivery system for cannabinoids should be developed.

The negative side effect profile for marijuana, even oral
dronabinol (Marinol®), far exceeds most of the other effective
agents available. *If* there exist treatment failures of available
medications in these patients, the use of marijuana would, at
minimum, demonstrate unpleasant side effects. In the studies
performed to examine THC for chemotherapy-associated nausea, elderly patients could not tolerate the drug. Chronic, daily
doses of the drug would be necessary to treat many of the proposed medical conditions. This would unnecessarily expose the
patients to the toxic effects. . . .

In 1997 the White House Office of National Drug Control
Policy commissioned the National Academy of Sciences Institute of Medicine (IOM) to undertake an evaluation of the utility of marijuana and other cannabinoids for medicinal applications. The study concluded that the challenge for future
research will be to find cannabinoids which enhance therapeutic benefits while minimizing side effects such as intoxication
and dysphoria [depression]. Delivery systems such as nasal
sprays, metered dose inhalers, transdermal patches, and sup-
positories could be useful delivery systems for isolated or synthetic cannabinoids. The future for medicinal applications of
cannabinoids and whether cannabinoids are equal or superior
to existing medicines remains to be determined. . . .

High Potential for Abuse

Marijuana adversely impacts concentration, motor coordination, and memory, factors that must be considered in any discussion of providing this drug to patients suffering chronic diseases. The ability to perform complex tasks, such as flying, is
impaired even 24 hours after the acute intoxication phase. The
association of marijuana use with trauma and intoxicated motor vehicle operation is also well established. This is of central
importance in an ambulatory environment where patients may
smoke marijuana and then drive automobiles. Recent evalua-

tions of the effect of marijuana on driving determined that . . . "Under marijuana's influence, drivers have reduced capacity to avoid collisions if confronted with the sudden need for evasive action." A . . . study found that a BAC of .05 combined with moderate marijuana produced a significant drop in the visual search frequency.

> *Marijuana adversely impairs some aspects of lung function and causes abnormalities in the respiratory cell linings.*

Despite arguments of the legalization advocates to the contrary, marijuana is a dependence-producing drug. Strangely, in the course of the rescheduling hearings, petitioners admitted that "marijuana has a high potential for abuse and that abuse of the marijuana plant may lead to severe psychological or physical dependence." These are points which they now deny. However, this dependence and associated "addictive" behaviors have been well described in the marijuana literature. Marijuana dependence consists of both a physical dependence (tolerance and subsequent withdrawal) and a psychological dependence. Withdrawal from marijuana has been demonstrated in both animals and humans.

While the dependence-producing properties of marijuana are probably a minimal issue for chemotherapy-associated nausea when medication is required sporadically, it is a major issue for the chronic daily use necessary for glaucoma, AIDS wasting syndrome, and other alleged chronic applications.

The respiratory difficulties associated with marijuana use preclude the inhaled route of administration as a medicine. Smoking marijuana is associated with higher concentrations of tar, carbon monoxide, and carcinogens than are found in cigarette smoking. Marijuana adversely impairs some aspects of lung function and causes abnormalities in the respiratory cell linings from large airways to the alveoli. Marijuana smoke causes inflammatory changes that are similar to the effects of tobacco in the airways of young people. In addition to these cellular abnormalities and consequences, contaminants of marijuana smoke are known to include various pathogenic bacteria and fungi. Those at particular risk for the development of disease and infection when these substances are inhaled are those users with impaired immunity.

One of the earliest findings in marijuana research was the effect on various immune functions, which is now evidenced by an inability to fight herpes infections and the discovery of a blunted response to therapy for genital warts during cannabis consumption. Abnormal immune function is, of course, the cornerstone of problems associated with AIDS. The use of chronic THC in smoked form for AIDS wasting not only exposes the patient to unnecessary pathogens, but also risks further immunosuppression. . . .

A hallmark of the treatment for AIDS is *avoidance* of drug use, not extension or perpetuation of it. It should be clear that marijuana exposes the user to substantial health risks. In chronic use, or use in populations at high risk for infection and immune suppression, the risks are unacceptable. . . .

In the interest of protecting seriously and terminally ill patients from unsafe and ineffective drugs, the safety and efficacy process of the FDA cannot be bypassed. Crude marijuana, an impure and toxic substance has no place in the [practice of medicine]. It is no more reasonable to consider marijuana a medicine than it is to consider tobacco a medicine.

Coupled with the medical risk to patients, serious regulatory questions arise that have not been adequately dealt with by ballot initiatives. Those who propose medical uses, or who conduct research on the use of marijuana, have an ethical responsibility not to expose their subjects to unnecessary risks. Under current guidelines, crude marijuana is not a medicine, and allowing it as such would be a step backward to the times of potions and herbal remedies.

12

Legalizing Ecstasy Could Help Psychotherapists Treat Patients

David Adams and Ben Fulton

David Adams is a feature writer for the Salt Lake City Weekly. *Ben Fulton is a writer and editor at the same newspaper.*

The drug MDMA, or Ecstasy, which is useful to people suffering from various psychological conditions, has been illegal since 1987. Used in a therapeutic setting Ecstasy has been shown to offer emotional release to those who have suffered deep trauma, such as sexual assault or torture. Unfortunately those in need of Ecstasy therapy must acquire the drug on their own, from street dealers, or from illegal small-scale producers. In 2004, the Food and Drug Administration (FDA) gave initial approval to Ecstasy research on a limited basis. While this is a positive step, the government should make the drug readily available to psychiatrists and psychologists who work with the most distressed patients.

S itting on a couch is Melissa, a woman in her mid-20s who has just taken 125 mg of methylenedioxymethamphetamine (MDMA), or ecstasy, in a glass of juice. Sitting in a rocking chair to the left of Melissa is licensed psychotherapist Dr. Jane, who will work intensely with her patient over the next few hours, as Melissa's brain bathes in the surplus neurochemicals brought on by the MDMA.

Melissa and her therapist aren't part of any currently approved research. They consider themselves to be conscientious, law-abiding citizens, but have decided to augment traditional psychotherapy with what the U.S. Drug Enforcement Administration [DEA] currently classifies as a Schedule I substance—an illegal drug [according to the federal Controlled Substances Act of 1970].

But, illegal or not, Dr. Jane (not her real name) has a rationale for using this drug with her patient: MDMA eases anxiety surrounding traumatic events, allowing them to be recalled with extensive clarity, then amplified by a desire to discuss them, perhaps for the first time in the patient's life.

Dr. Jane is one of an informal network of a half dozen or so psychologists—licensed social workers and psychiatrists practicing [in Utah]—with the experience and willingness to work with patients who choose to use MDMA in conjunction with other drug-free therapy sessions.

> **//** With its relatively minimal side effects, therapists classified the drug as an 'empathogen' for its ability to open the heart, increase awareness and foster sensations of self-love and acceptance. **//**

She and her underground clinical colleagues aren't doing anything new. Long before its popularity blossomed under the moniker of "ecstasy" in dance clubs and warehouses across Europe and North America, and long after its first patent by German pharmaceutical company Merck in 1914, MDMA was used by scores of psychotherapists during the 1970s and halfway through the 1980s. With its relatively minimal side effects, therapists classified the drug as an "empathogen" for its ability to open the heart, increase awareness and foster sensations of self-love and acceptance. In addition, the drug has the added benefit of keeping the patient firmly grounded and in control, rather than orbiting Pluto as occurs with stronger drugs. From the perspective of the analyst's chair, these are all very desirable traits.

From its ingestion, MDMA takes about 45 minutes to take effect. During this time, Melissa nods her head in affirmation, as Dr. Jane reads aloud the goals for this session and the safety contract, both of which have been developed and agreed upon during six earlier preparation sessions.

It is now 60 minutes past the point when Melissa unwrapped a small triangle of tinfoil, emptied the white, powdered contents into a glass of juice and drank it down in one long gulp. Her earlier, tense posture has given way to a more relaxed position on the doctor's leather couch. The pillow she had been clutching nervously in her lap is now resting under her right leg, and her head rests gently on the back of the sofa. Melissa is both alert, and noticeably relaxed, as she talks openly about abuse that occurred early in her childhood. Dr. Jane listens intently, only occasionally asking questions that probe lightly into progressively deeper layers of [Melissa's] memories.

Now two hours into her session, tears fall from Melissa's face and into a white Kleenex she holds in her hand as she recounts one particularly strong memory. Using a succession of questions, Dr. Jane assists Melissa in understanding how her earlier trauma caused her to project certain beliefs into her present relationships—beliefs that are creating some problems.

Towards the end of her session Melissa says: "Reliving this incident helped me free up my emotions in a number of ways; I know that I have a lot more to do, but I know now that I molded my views about the world—that I now know are not true—because that one incident caused me to distrust my parents."

Melissa, who works as a computer programmer, seems visibly relieved, and hopeful. Weeks after the sessions, she sent a promised e-mail describing the sum of her three MDMA-assisted therapy sessions: "I was able to dump my file; the medicine cleared my channels; insights and memories poured through me; fragments and pieces of the puzzle all came together. I had a cloud of trauma that had seemed in front of me [and] that for almost my whole life had been distorting my beliefs about myself, it seems, behind me now, and I've gotten a new sense of who I am."

Serious Psychotherapy

Don't rush out to your local psychotherapist for sessions on the couch with this "love drug" just yet, though. First of all, these renegade therapists will allow only certain patients to use the drug, and only after a careful screening and analysis process of several therapy sessions in advance of taking the drug. The

91

drug's therapeutic effects have been found especially beneficial to those suffering from post-traumatic stress disorder (PTSD).

Second, don't go thinking that your time on the couch will amount to some sort of drug-crazed party of one. Most patients take MDMA during therapy twice at least, maybe three times at most. Perhaps most discouraging of all is the fact that you will have to score the drug yourself. Patients who desire this type of therapy assume all the responsibility in obtaining, possessing and ingesting the drug. Finding authentic MDMA, free of adulterants and of known strength, takes some work, but is not difficult. Dr. Jane cautions any prospective MDMA patient against running down to the local warehouse or club to buy a hit from a raver sporting an X on his shirt. You're more likely to end up with a fake drug or sometimes-harmful counterfeit. Some have had luck procuring legitimate samples from undergraduate chemistry students who've figured out that MDMA is not all that difficult to synthesize.

> **MAPS . . .** *launched a '$5 million, five-year Clinical Plan' to one day see MDMA made into a prescription drug for the treatment of post-traumatic stress disorder.*

Once the patient procures the drug, Dr. Jane provides guidance on determining [the] potency of the MDMA, and assists with dosing. Preparation sessions are crucial. Not only are patients given information on the risks and benefits of therapy using the drug, they also establish goals for the session, discuss expectations, and how information yielded during the MDMA session will be integrated in the patient's life. Dr. Jane follows a safety protocol that involves having a trusted friend or relative assume charge [of] the patient after the session, among other things.

In short, MDMA-assisted psychotherapy is serious business, not a dance party for which it's commonly used. Those who take the drug recreationally to enhance the repetitive beat of dance music and feel closer to other people at a party will gain a few pleasant hours with little or no insight into themselves. An MDMA session in the confines of an office and under the guidance of an experienced professional is something else entirely.

Before the drug was criminalized in 1985, Rick Doblin, an expert on the therapeutic and medical uses of marijuana and psychedelics who earned his doctorate from Harvard University's Kennedy School of Government, was witness to MDMA's effects on patients during psychotherapy. "I saw first hand just how helpful it was for certain patients," he said during a telephone interview from his Boston home.

> *It's very possible that if the government said this was a good drug for therapy, fewer people would be enticed by its illegal status.*

But as the drug gained more and more publicity for its pleasurable qualities at dance and club parties, as opposed to its less sensational benefits during psychotherapy, the DEA moved to ban the drug under Schedule I classification. Therapists protested, suing the government in court. An administrative law judge agreed that the drug shouldn't be classified as such but could only make a recommendation to the DEA. The agency said, in effect, "Thanks, but no thanks." As if to buttress the DEA's position, the scientific community released study after study questioning the drug's safety and long-term effects. The most damning studies, by Johns Hopkins University researcher Dr. George A. Ricaurte, concluded that MDMA use leads to permanent brain damage in primates and damaged the brain's dopamine neurons. Upping the fear factor, the doctor also concluded that use of the drug could lead to Parkinson's disease in humans. But in a stunning reversal, Ricaurte himself put those findings to rest [in] September 2003 when he admitted in *Science* magazine that his researchers had not given primates used in his studies MDMA, but another drug entirely [methamphetamine]. However, even some of Ricaurte's detractors say his earlier studies demonstrating the drug's neurotoxic qualities may have merit. Debate about the drug's long-term effects continues, but many hope that with Ricaurte's primate study now invalidated, a new era of study surrounding the drug's benefits will soon dawn. About time, too, they say.

Doblin founded the Multi-Disciplinary Association for Psychedelic Studies (MAPS) in 1986 with just that goal in mind. Based in Sarasota, Fla., his organization works to advance the study of MDMA's therapeutic value through legitimate scientific studies. The United States isn't the only nation with resistance to studying the drug's therapeutic uses. Spain hosted the first scientific study of MDMA in the world, testing its therapeutic value on women survivors of sexual assault. The study seemed to be advancing quite well according to media reports. Then the International Narcotics Control Board shut it down.

Although there is considerable anecdotal evidence about the benefits of MDMA-assisted therapy, scientific confirmation of its effectiveness is admittedly minimal. The most notable of the few studies originate from a group of Swiss psychiatrists who used MDMA in conjunction with psychotherapy from 1988 to 1993. During the six-year period, 121 patients underwent a total of 818 sessions. More than 90 percent of the patients described themselves as "significantly improved." During the course of the study, there were no adverse incidents, no suicides, no psychiatric hospitalizations and no negative reactions.

FDA Approves Research

Doblin's MAPS is working hard to change the drug's research landscape. It launched a "$5 million, five-year Clinical Plan" to one day see MDMA made into a prescription drug for the treatment of post-traumatic stress disorder. The organization is also trying to secure funding for research at Harvard University, where the drug might be tested on advanced cancer patients to help mitigate their fear of death and other anxieties, Doblin said. But the truly big news among MDMA's proponents was the FDA's November 2001 green light for a study of the drug's effects on people with PTSD. . . . In February [2004] the proposed study also earned necessary regulatory approval from the DEA. Together, both approvals mark the first time since the drug was criminalized that it will officially be studied for therapeutic value.

For Doblin, this kind of approval for scientific study of MDMA makes the perfect bookmark to 1963, when [then-professor] Timothy Leary got the boot from Harvard University for his studies regarding LSD. "The Israelites, so to speak, have been wandering in the desert for 40 years. Researchers have been locked out of the lab, wandering the wilderness for that long. It's really the first time in decades that we've had any research on these substances at all," he said. "The quest for verification and scientific research is totally appropriate. What's fundamentally problematic is that it's taken us so long to even get to that point. It's especially difficult to gain traditional funding sources for this kind of research, too. The drug is just too controversial for them to even touch it."

All this is extremely important news for therapists like Dr. Jane, too. A practicing psychotherapist in Salt Lake City for years, one of the degrees on her wall boasts the blue and white accents of a relatively conservative Utah school. Displayed on the wall just below that degree is a license issued by the Utah Department of Occupational Licensing to practice as a clinical psychologist. She's gravely aware that her license and livelihood could be in jeopardy each time a patient of hers takes MDMA under her supervision. One patient with one bad reaction is about all that separates her from a bee's nest of legal problems, investigators, and a trip (no pun intended) in front of the licensing board.

Nevertheless, she is resolute. "I would rather tender my license and make widgets than turn a blind, fearful eye away from an avenue of treatment that may help someone," she said. "MDMA has a fantastic ability to scan through the unconscious, lock onto areas of emotional tension, and then allow the patient to talk about themselves in spite of any defensive walls they've created."

Like her patient Melissa, the Utah doctor has her own description of MDMA-assisted therapy: "Feelings of self-love and self-acceptance suffuse the session and, frequently, they can endure long after the drug has left the body," she said. And any good psychotherapist knows that any long-lasting behavioral change has its roots in feelings of genuine self-love.

People ask me all the time if I can refer them to therapists [using MDMA], and I cannot. I know it's going on, but I don't know exactly who's doing it. I know they're out there."

Those are the words of Julie Holland, M.D. A New York University psychiatry professor and psychiatrist in practice [in] Greenwich Village, she's widely considered the most celebrated authority regarding MDMA's therapeutic value. And with Ricaurte's studies discredited, her comments are no longer seen as those of the naive proponent. Just ask *Newsweek*, and other publications in which her words have gotten a forum. Taking a break from vacation in Massachusetts to speak by phone, her voice is measured and assured, even if occasionally surprised.

"You found some underground therapists? That's great, and it's not easy to do," she said.

Anyone who's ever heard of [the antidepressant] Prozac or lithium [used in the treatment of bipolar disorder] knows that the marriage of drugs and therapy is nothing new. That's one of the reasons Holland has no qualms about entertaining the use of MDMA with patients on the couch. She seems shocked that anyone would consider its use such a radical departure. In addition to authoring an exhaustive research paper on the drug, she edited articles by 21 of the world's most noted MDMA experts, compiled in 2001 under the title *Ecstasy: The Complete Guide.*

One of Holland's favorite quotes from an article included in her book comes from George Greer, a therapist who prescribed the drug for patients while it was legal, only to find himself forced to stop using it. "I felt like an artist who'd just discovered oil paints, but had to put them away and start using charcoal again because people were sniffing the oil paint," Greer wrote.

Holland sympathizes with any physician forced to put effective medicine aside. And she believes MDMA can be especially beneficial, not just for people with PTSD, but also with adults who were physically or sexually abused as children. "Psychiatry doesn't really have many good tools in its armament when you get right down to it. This is a really good tool," she said. "And it's very possible that if the government said this was a good drug for therapy, fewer people would be enticed by its illegal status."

The irony of recent FDA and DEA decisions to approve preliminary studies of the drug, however, is that now government seems to have taken the lead where universities and private companies haven't taken the trouble. Universities, of course, are cautious to do anything that smacks of illegality. But the reason why corporations never took MDMA's case before the FDA or DEA is clear, Holland believes. "No pharmaceutical company has gotten behind this because [MDMA's] patent is expired, and it's a drug that the average patient will take once or twice during therapy, and that's it. There's no profit margin in it," she said.

Similar to Prozac

But that doesn't mean there's no connection between current favorites such as Prozac and MDMA. Both drugs work to release [the neurotransmitter] serotonin, which brings on a general sense of openness, energy and well-being. But where Prozac merely stops the recycling of serotonin, so that it backs up in the brain to make more available for the synapses, MDMA, on the other hand, floods the brain with serotonin. In addition, like Prozac, it also stops the recycling, or uptake, of serotonin as well.

Once again, this isn't the party drug you may have heard of. You're certainly not dancing to loud music in psychotherapy. No, you're talking about potentially painful events in your life.

"It's a very subtle experience. For most people it's about as subtle as having one or two glasses of wine," Holland said. "It's not as big of a break from normal consciousness as people might think it is. But give it a name like Ecstasy and people have a lot of assumptions about it.

> *In a way, MDMA is the anti-drug, because Prozac and Zoloft are drugs people have to take every day, and when people stop taking them their problems come back.*

"It's similar to anesthesia during surgery. It's not that you're pain-free, but you are very much more relaxed. You have to really peel through layers of defenses to get to core therapy. People are pretty much laid out, and you're much more likely to get to the malignant core of what's going on. It allows you to more readily examine it, and potentially excise it or remove it. It makes therapy much more efficient and effective. You don't have to spend three years building an alliance with your therapist. It really strengthens that alliance, which is really important for future sessions."

And unlike alcohol or other sedatives that would result in blurry disinhibition, MDMA has the added benefit of letting a patient recall the experience of what was discussed. That's due to the drug's amphetamine base, which gives patients greater ability to remember what's happened. And when an issue is recalled and remembered, there's no need to talk about it over and over. Taken once or twice during therapy, Holland said, MDMA can reap multiple benefits in future sessions.

Doblin concurs. "In a way, MDMA is the anti-drug, because Prozac and [antidepressant, antianxiety agent] Zoloft are drugs people have to take every day, and when people stop taking them their problems come back," he points out. "MDMA in therapy is taken only a few times. In the PTSD study, people take it only twice. It was never intended to be a regular daily drug in a therapeutic setting, and was never intended to be a take-home drug."

Concern over the drug's current status as an illegal substance is that it may sit forever in the recreational realm, where it's most often used incorrectly. Used in the context of a dance party, users frequently experience dehydration, overheating or elevated blood pressure. Used in psychotherapy and under professional supervision, those conditions are much less likely to occur.

"Millions of people around the world are using it recreationally; it gets more popular every year," Holland said. "But people who could really benefit from it, can't. It's a real tragedy and a real shame.". . .

But in consideration of the universal side effects described by the millions of people who've used the drug, MDMA's major risks to any individual appear to be the very real possibility of being arrested and jailed.

Still, even proponents such as Doblin know the importance of research, whether that be to prove the drug's effectiveness, or demonstrate its risks. "That's one of the lessons we learned from the '60s," Doblin said. "You can't downplay the risks or emphasize the benefits.". . .

If, and when, MAPS provides the FDA with sufficient evidence of MDMA's usefulness and it's approved as a prescription medication, adults suffering from emotional problems will have the option to walk into a local clinic and receive the drug in a setting conducive to healing.

For his part, Doblin roots for any [Utah] psychotherapist brave enough to blaze such a trail while the drug remains illegal. "I feel a lot of sympathy and pride that there are . . . people in Utah who care enough about their patients that they're willing to risk their freedom and licenses," he said. "That creates a lot of inspiration and responsibility in me to work even harder to see this through."

13

Efforts to Prove That Ecstasy Can Help Psychotherapists Treat Patients Are Misguided

E. Patrick Curry

E. Patrick Curry is a retired computer specialist who is interested in exposing the inadequacy of the scientific backing of many of the claims of those advocating for alternative medicine. He has written for the Scientific Review of Alternative Medicine *and received the 2000 Scientific and Professional Integrity Trophy from* The Science & Pseudoscience Review in Mental Health.

The Food and Drug Administration (FDA) made a mistake when it approved the use of Ecstasy, or MDMA, in 2004. Research has shown the drug to cause brain damage and other problems. By giving it to patients suffering from psychological trauma, Ecstasy proponents are violating ethical rules concerning drug research on human volunteers. Those who have been given permission to conduct the research have promoted the widespread use of drugs such as LSD in the past. They have an obvious bias when it comes to Ecstasy research and are not using accepted scientific parameters in their studies. MDMA is a dangerous substance that should not be classified as a therapeutic drug. The FDA should call off this study now before research subjects are permanently injured.

The editors of two journals that provide objective scientific investigations of controversial and largely untested medical and mental health practices have criticized proposed research using the drug MDMA (Ecstasy) as a treatment for posttraumatic stress disorder [PTSD]. The study, "MDMA-Assisted Psychotherapy in the Treatment of Posttraumatic Stress Disorder", is awaiting final MDMA licensing approval from the Drug Enforcement Administration.

Proponents from the Multidisciplinary Association for Psychedelic Studies (MAPS) claim that it will prove that MDMA has strong potential as a psychotherapeutic drug. The President of MAPS, Rick Doblin, is a long time proponent of recreational and spiritual use of both LSD and Ecstasy. The protocol was developed in the Charleston, S.C., area with the assistance of MAPS. The proposed study subjects would be 20 victims of violent assault who have been given diagnoses of posttraumatic stress disorder.

MDMA has recently received national attention because of research published in the journal *Science*, implicating MDMA in damage to dopamine receptors in mammalian brains. Reductions in [the neurotransmitter] dopamine are associated with Parkinson's disease. Although the precise neurological effects of Ecstasy remain controversial in the scientific community, there is a widespread consensus that this drug has the potential to do harm in at least certain cases.

Editors Scott Lilienfeld, Ph.D., of the *Scientific Review of Mental Health Practice* and Wallace Sampson, MD, of the *Scientific Review of Alternative Medicine*, based on detailed investigations by health advocate E. Patrick Curry, note that the research was approved by the Food and Drug Administration (FDA) in late 2001 and by the independent Western Institutional Review Board in July [2002]. In light of reports of damaging effects of MDMA, the [doctors] found the research to be potentially dangerous and possibly in violation of human subjects research ethical standards. They also note that evidence for effectiveness that would justify such research was lacking.

Flawed Studies

According to Lilienfeld, an Associate Professor of Psychology at Emory University [in Atlanta] and President of the Society for a Science of Clinical Psychology, the study itself is scientifically questionable at best and meaningless at worst, because the treatment will not be compared with a meaningful and properly blinded control group consisting of either no therapy or a comparison treatment of known effectiveness. Lilienfeld stated: "Because the overt physiological and subjective psychological effects of MDMA will be evident to most or all participants in the study and to the investigators, it will essentially be impossible for either researchers or participants to remain blind to treatment condition. As a consequence, the findings of the study will be methodologically flawed and therefore essentially uninterpretable."

> **❝ [Doctors] found the [Ecstasy] research to be potentially dangerous and possibly in violation of human subjects research ethical standards. ❞**

"One of the most disturbing things about this study," Dr. Sampson continued, "is that it appears to be the exclusive project of believers in psychedelic mysticism, and based on work of Dr. Stanislav Grof, an early LSD self-experimenter and psychedelic psychotherapist. After LSD and Ecstasy use was declared illegal, Grof developed Holotropic Breathwork, a potentially dangerous form of severe hyperventilation, as a legal method of invoking hallucinations. Grof was a long time fellow of the Esalen Institute, widely considered to be a birthplace of the New Age movement. MAPS President Doblin, whose organization is funding the PTSD research, was first introduced to MDMA personally by Grof at Esalen in the early 1980s. . . ."

Both therapists involved in the research, principal investigator Dr. Michael Mithoefer and his wife, Ann Mithoefer, a psychiatric nurse, are trained practitioners of Grof's Holotropic Breathwork. The investigators' background, although not bearing directly on the methodological quality of the study, raises troubling questions concerning the investigators' capacity to conduct the research and to evaluate the data impartially without strong a priori [previously assumed] allegiances.

Drs. Sampson and Lilienfeld question how such an experiment was approved by the FDA and an Institutional Review Board [IRB]. Efforts by MAPS and the principal investigator, Dr. Mithoefer to win IRB support from the Medical University of South Carolina were rebuffed [in 2002]. The project was approved within weeks when submitted to the independent IRB.

Sampson and Lilienfeld concur that comments in the popular press presenting this Charleston study as a possible "tie-breaker" in the debate over the effects of MDMA are misplaced. Prof. Lilienfeld states "it is disturbing that scientifically flawed and potentially dangerous research like this could pass muster with the FDA, an IRB, and popular journalism."

Organizations to Contact

The editors have compiled the following list of organizations concerned with the issues debated in this book. The descriptions are derived from materials provided by the organizations. All have publications or information available for interested readers. The list was compiled on the date of publication of the present volume; names, addresses, phone and fax numbers, and e-mail addresses may change. Be aware that many organizations take several weeks or longer to respond to inquiries, so allow as much time as possible.

American Civil Liberties Union (ACLU)
125 Broad St., 18th Fl., New York, NY 10004-2400
(212) 549-2500
e-mail: aclu@aclu.org • Web site: www.aclu.org

The ACLU is a national organization that works to defend civil rights guaranteed by the Constitution. The organization has been challenging the constitutionality of the laws behind the drug war in court since the 1980s and publishes various materials on drugs and other civil liberties issues, including the newsletter *Civil Liberties* and a set of handbooks on individual rights.

American Council for Drug Education (ACDE)
164 W. Seventy-fourth St., New York, NY 10023
(800) 488-DRUG (3784) • fax: (212) 595-2553
e-mail: acde@phoenixhouse.org • Web site: www.acde.org

The American Council for Drug Education informs the public about the harmful effects of abusing drugs and alcohol. It gives the public access to scientifically based, compelling prevention programs and materials. ACDE has resources for parents, youth, educators, prevention professionals, employers, health care professionals, and other concerned community members who are working to help America's youth avoid the dangers of drug and alcohol abuse.

Cato Institute
1000 Massachusetts Ave. NW, Washington, DC 20001-5403
(202) 842-0200 • fax: (202) 842-3490
e-mail: jblock@cato.org • Web site: www.cato.org

The Cato Institute is a nonprofit libertarian public policy research foundation headquartered in Washington, D.C. The institute seeks to broaden the parameters of public policy debate to allow consideration of the traditional American principles of limited government, individual liberty, free markets, and opposition to the war on drugs. The institute researches issues in the media and provides commentary for magazine, newspaper, and news program editorials. It publishes *Regulation* magazine.

Drug Enforcement Administration (DEA)
2401 Jefferson Davis Hwy., Mailstop AXS, Alexandria, VA 22301
(202) 305-8500
Web site: www.dea.gov

The mission of the Drug Enforcement Administration is to enforce the controlled substances laws and regulations of the United States and bring to the criminal and civil justice system of the United States those involved in the growing, manufacture, or distribution of controlled substances. The DEA also recommends and supports nonenforcement measures such as public education programs aimed at reducing the availability of illicit controlled substances on the domestic and international markets. The DEA provides information about illicit drugs on its Web site.

Drug Policy Alliance
925 Fifteenth St. NW, 2nd Fl., Washington, DC 20005
(202) 216-0035 • fax: (202) 216-0803
e-mail: dc@drugpolicy.org • Web site: www.drugpolicy.org

Drug Policy Alliance is the leading organization working to broaden the public debate on drug policy and to promote alternatives to the war on drugs based on science, compassion, health, and human rights. The alliance is guided by the belief that steps can and should be taken to reduce the harms associated with both drug use and the drug war, including making marijuana legally available for medical purposes; curtailing drug testing; redirecting most government drug control resources from criminal justice and interdiction to public health and education; supporting effective, science-based drug education and ending support for ineffective programs; and repealing mandatory minimum sentences for nonviolent drug offenses. The online Drug Policy Alliance library is one of the largest collections on drugs and drug policy in the world. It contains over ten thousand books, reports, government documents, periodicals, videos, and articles from the United States and abroad as well as in-depth collections on drug-related policies in Canada, Latin America, and European nations.

Drug Reform Coordination Network (DRCNet)
1623 Connecticut Ave. NW, 3rd Fl., Washington, DC 20009
(202) 293-8340 • fax: (202) 293-8344
e-mail: drcnet@drcnet.org • Web site: www.stopthedrugwar.org

The Drug Reform Coordination Network was founded in 1993 and has grown into a major national and global network, including parents, educators, students, lawyers, health care professionals, academics, and others working for drug policy reform from a variety of perspectives, including harm reduction, reform of sentencing and forfeiture laws, medicalization of current Schedule I drugs such as marijuana and Ecstasy, and promotion of an open debate on drug prohibition. DRCNet opposes the prison-building industry and supports policies consistent with the principles of peace, justice, freedom, compassion, and truth. The network's online drug policy library contains hundreds of documents relating to drug prohibition. It also publishes a weekly newsletter, *Drug War Chronicle*, available through e-mail subscription.

Law Enforcement Against Prohibition (LEAP)
27 Austin Rd., Medford, MA 02155
e-mail: info@leap.cc • Web site: www.leap.cc

The membership of Law Enforcement Against Prohibition is composed primarily of current and former members of law enforcement. LEAP members believe that to save lives and lower the rates of disease, crime, and addiction, as well as to conserve tax dollars, drug prohibition must end. Jointly, the members of LEAP have had a great deal of experience in first advancing U.S. drug policy goals and then in trying to change those policies. That experience includes many years of working as police officers to arrest drug-law violators and to keep drugs from being smuggled into the country; disenchantment with and in-depth reconsideration of those policies; and speaking out to alert the public, media, and policy makers to the global harms resulting from the U.S. policy of drug prohibition. The organization Friends of LEAP was created for those who have never been part of law enforcement but who wish to support the group's work of ending prohibition. LEAP's Web site contains many articles about drug legalization.

National Center on Addiction and Substance Abuse at Columbia University (CASA).
633 Third Ave., 19th Fl., New York, NY 10017-6706
(212) 841-5200 • fax: (212) 956-8020
Web site: www.casacolumbia.org

CASA is a private nonprofit organization that works to educate the public about the costs and hazards of substance abuse and the prevention and treatment of all forms of chemical dependency. The center supports treatment as the best way to reduce chemical dependency. The Policy Research and Analysis Division of CASA produces publications such as *Family Matters: Substance Abuse and the American Family*, describing the harmful effects of alcohol and drug addiction and effective ways to address the problem of substance abuse.

National Families in Action
2957 Clairmont Rd. NE, Suite 150, Atlanta, GA 30329
(404) 248-9676 • fax: (404) 248-1312
e-mail: nfia@nationalfamilies.org • Web site: www.nationalfamilies.org

National Families in Action was founded in Atlanta, Georgia, in 1977. Its mission is to help families and communities prevent drug use among children by promoting policies based on science. To further its mission, the organization makes a variety of documents available on its Web site, including pamphlets, brochures, resource guides, news updates, newspaper editorials, book excerpts, and other publications with an antidrug message.

National Institute on Drug Abuse (NIDA)
6001 Executive Blvd., Room 5213, Bethesda, MD 20892-9561
(301) 443-1124
e-mail: information@lists.nida.nih.gov • Web site: www.nida.nih.gov

NIDA's mission is to use the power of science to stop drug abuse and addiction. In its mission, NIDA supports over 85 percent of the world's research on the health aspects of drug abuse and addiction. This support addresses the most fundamental and essential questions about drug abuse, ranging from the molecule to managed care and from DNA to community outreach research. NIDA is not only seizing upon unprecedented opportunities and technologies to further understand how drugs of abuse affect the brain and behavior, but is also working to ensure the rapid and effective transfer of scientific data to policy makers, drug abuse and other health care practitioners, and the general public. The organization's publications catalog is available online and contains documents relating to basic research, the nature and extent of drug abuse, causes of drug abuse and addiction, HIV/AIDS, drug abuse treatment, and preventing drug abuse.

National Organization for the Reform of Marijuana Laws (NORML)
1600 K St. NW, Suite 501, Washington, DC 20006-2832
(202) 483-5500 • fax: (202) 483-0057
e-mail: norml@norml.org • Web site: www.norml.org

Since its founding in 1970 NORML has provided a voice in the public policy debate for those Americans who oppose marijuana prohibition and favor an end to the practice of arresting marijuana smokers. A nonprofit public-interest advocacy group, NORML represents the interests of the tens of millions of Americans who smoke marijuana responsibly. NORML continues to lead the fight to reform state and federal marijuana laws, whether by voter initiative or through the elected legislatures. NORML serves as an informational resource to the national media on marijuana-related stories, providing a perspective to offset the antimarijuana message of the government. The organization publishes two newsletters, the *Legislative Bulletin* and *Leaflet*, available by subscription or through the group's Web site.

Partnership for a Drug-Free America (PDFA)
405 Lexington Ave., Suite 1601, New York, NY 10174
(212) 922-1560 • fax: (212) 922-1570
e-mail: webmail@drugfree.org • Web site: www.drugfreeamerica.org

The Partnership for a Drug-Free America is a nonprofit coalition of professionals from the communications industry. Through its national drug education advertising campaign and other forms of media communication, the partnership exists to help kids and teens reject substance abuse by influencing attitudes through persuasive information. With deep roots in the advertising industry, the partnership is composed of a small staff and hundreds of volunteers from the communications industry, who create and disseminate the partnership's work. National research suggests that the partnership's national advertising campaign—the largest public service campaign in the history of advertising—has played a contributing role in reducing overall drug use in America. PDFA offers a variety of e-newsletters for parents and caregivers, teens and young adults, those in treatment/recovery, and a semiannual digest that summarizes the group's work.

Bibliography

Books

David C. Cole	*No Equal Justice: Race and Class in the American Criminal Justice System.* New York: New Press, 1999.
David T. Courtwright	*Forces of Habit: Drugs and the Making of the Modern World.* Cambridge, MA: Harvard University Press, 2001.
Richard Davenport-Hines	*The Pursuit of Oblivion: A Global History of Narcotics.* New York: Norton, 2002.
Steven B. Duke and Albert C. Gross	*America's Longest War: Rethinking Our Tragic Crusade Against Drugs.* New York: Putnam, 1993.
James P. Gray	*Why Our Drug Laws Have Failed and What We Can Do About It: A Judicial Indictment of Our War on Drugs.* Philadelphia: Temple University Press, 2001.
Mike Gray, ed.	*Busted: Stone Cowboys, Narco-Lords, and Washington's War on Drugs.* New York: Thunder's Mouth/ Nation, 2002.
Douglas N. Husak	*Legalize This! The Case for Decriminalizing Drugs.* New York: Verso, 2002.
James A. Inciardi	*The War on Drugs III.* Boston: Allyn and Bacon, 2002.
James A. Inciardi and Lana D. Harrison, eds.	*Harm Reduction: National and International Perspectives.* Thousand Oaks, CA: Sage, 2000.
Jesse L. Jackson Jr.	*A More Perfect Union: Advancing New American Rights.* New York: Welcome Rain, 2001.
Clarence Lusane	*Pipe Dream Blues: Racism and the War on Drugs.* Boston: South End Press, 1991.
Tim Lynch, ed.	*After Prohibition: An Adult Approach to Drug Policies in the 21st Century.* Washington, DC: CATO, 2000.
Marc Mauer	*Race to Incarcerate.* New York: New Press, 1999.
George McMahon and Christopher Largen	*Prescription Pot: A Leading Advocate's Heroic Battle to Legalize Medical Marijuana.* Far Hills, NJ: New Horizon, 2003.
Jerome G. Miller	*Search and Destroy: African-American Males in the Criminal Justice System.* New York: Cambridge University Press, 1996.
National Research Council for the Office of National Drug Control Policy	*Informing America's Policy on Illegal Drugs: What We Don't Know Keeps Hurting Us.* Washington, DC: National Academy Press, 2001.

Preston Peet, ed.	*Under the Influence: The Disinformation Guide to Drugs.* San Leandro, CA: Disinformation Company, 2004.
Michael Pollan	*The Botany of Desire: A Plant's-Eye View of the World.* New York: Random House, 2001.
Jeffrey A. Schaler, ed.	*Drugs: Should We Legalize, Decriminalize or Deregulate?* Amherst, NY: Prometheus, 1998.
Eric Schlosser	*Reefer Madness: Sex, Drugs, and Cheap Labor in the American Black Market.* Boston: Houghton Mifflin, 2003.
Stuart Walton	*Out of It: A Cultural History of Intoxication.* New York: Harmony, 2002.
Lynn Zimmer and John Morgan	*Marijuana Myths, Marijuana Facts.* New York: Lindesmith Center, 1997.

Periodicals

Sasha Abramsky	"The Drug War Goes Up in Smoke: A Budget Crisis and a Prison Boom Make the States a Vanguard for Drug Reform," *Nation*, August 18, 2003.
Paul Armentano	"Bush's Born-Again Drug War," *AlterNet*, August 12, 2004. www.alternet.org/drugreporter/19547.
Christie Aschwanden	"Ecstasy for Agony?" *Health*, July/August 2002.
Sheerly Avni	"Ecstasy Begets Empathy," Salon.com, September 12, 2002.
R. Richard Banks	"Beyond Profiling: Race, Policing, and the Drug War," *Stanford Law Review*, December 2003.
Andrew Barr	"Altered States," *Wilson Quarterly*, Winter 2003.
Virginia Berridge	"Altered States: Opium and Tobacco Compared," *Social Research*, Fall 2001.
Daniel Chandler et al.	"Substance Abuse, Employment, and Welfare Tenure," *Social Service Review*, December 2004.
James A. Davis	"Did Growing Up in the 1960s Leave a Permanent Mark on Attitudes and Values? Evidence from the General Social Survey," *Public Opinion Quarterly*, Summer 2004.
Keith Donoghue	"Casualties of War: Criminal Drug Law Enforcement and Its Special Costs for the Poor," *New York University Law Review*, December 2002.
Michael Erard	"Open Secrets: How the Government Lost the Drug War in Cyberspace," *Reason*, October 2004.
Graham Farrell and David E. Carter	"Is the Drug War Over? The Declining Proportion of Drug Offenders," *Corrections Compendium*, February 2003.
Carlotta Grandstaff	"Putting Pot in Its Place," *Missoula (MT) Independent*, December 21, 2004.

Lester Grinspoon and Rick Doblin — "Psychedelics as Catalysts of Insight-Oriented Psychotherapy," *Social Research*, Fall 2001.

Asa Hutchinson — "An Effective Drug Policy to Protect America's Youth and Communities," *Fordham Urban Law Journal*, January 2003.

Alain Joffe and W. Samuel Yancy — "Legalization of Marijuana: Potential Impact on Youth," *Pediatrics*, June 2004.

Joseph E. Kennedy — "Drug Wars in Black and White," *Law and Contemporary Problems*, Summer 2003.

Richard Lowry — "Weed Whackers: The Anti-Marijuana Forces, and Why They're Wrong," *National Review*, August 20, 2001.

Donna Lyons — "Conviction for Addiction: States Are Reconsidering Whether No-Nonsense Drug Policy Should Mean Prison or Treatment," *State Legislatures*, June 2002.

Tony Mauro — "High Court Justice Rails About Evils of Mandatory Minimum Sentencing," *New Jersey Law Journal*, April 14, 2003.

Mike Miliard — "Up in Smoke," *Boston Phoenix*, December 16, 2004.

Paul Craig Roberts — "Constitution Is Drug War's Casualty," Townhall.com, August 1, 2001. www.townhall.

Randall G. Shelden — "Inside the Gulag: African Americans and Imprisonment for Drug Offenses," *Index on Censorship*, May/June 2001.

Robert Silbering — "The 'War on Drugs': A View from the Trenches," *Social Research*, Fall 2001.

Carla Spartos — "Ecstasy Therapy Is Back," *Village Voice*, January 8, 2002.

Brandon Spun — "Move Over Prozac, It's Ecstasy's Turn," *Insight on the News*, April 15, 2002.

Joel Stein — "The New Politics of Pot: Can It Go Legit?" *Time*, November 4, 2002.

Daniel Wolfe — "Condemned to Death: Thanks to the U.S.-Led Drug War, AIDS Is Exploding Among Injection Drug Users," *Nation*, April 26, 2004.

Index